Britain's Coming Energy Crisis

Peak Oil and the End of the World as we Know it

Tim Watkins

Waye Forward (Publishing) Ltd
Llanishen
Cardiff
CF14 5FA

ISBN-13: 978-0-9930877-3-8
ISBN-10: 0993087736

© Tim Watkins

CONTENTS

ABOUT THE AUTHOR

Tim Watkins is a founder-director of Waye Forward Ltd, a company established to support those individuals and businesses that have previously been unable to access professional design and publishing services.

Tim Watkins graduated from a Russell Group University with a First Class economics degree in 1990.

Between 1990 and 1997 he worked as a policy researcher with the Welsh Consumer Council where he wrote and published several key policy reports including: *Quality of Life and Quality of Service* - an investigation into the provision of residential care homes for older people - and *In Deep Water* - an investigation into the many problems that followed the North Wales (Towyn) floods of February 1990.

Between 1998 and 2010, Tim Watkins was employed by the charity Depression Alliance Cymru, initially as a development worker, and between 2003 and 2010 as its Director. During that time he produced several mental health publications for the charity.

Between 2001 and 2010 Tim Watkins was appointed to sit on several Welsh Government advisory bodies including the *Health and Wellbeing Council for Wales*, the *Burrows-Greenwell Review of Mental Health Services in Wales* and the *Expert Panel on Depression*.

After 2010, Tim Watkins has authored a range of mental health-related books and booklets, together with two books about charities.

A qualified Life Coach, he also provides coaching, mentoring and support to other writers.

Foreword

Had you talked to a Roman citizen at the height of the Roman Empire, he would have told you about the wonders of his civilisation. He would point to the enemies that had been vanquished and the territory that had been conquered. He would tell you about the technological developments – the roads, the aqueducts, underfloor heating, advanced mining techniques, literature, architecture and art. He would point to the benefits of trade within the Empire. He would tell you about improvements in literacy among the population. He would be horrified and offended were you to suggest that from this point on, the Empire would be in permanent decline. Nevertheless, we know that the Roman Empire did reach a peak before entering a prolonged downfall.

Since then we have witnessed the rise and fall of empires time and time again: Franks, Mongols, Angevins, Spanish, French, German, Russian, Japanese, and British (twice[1]) all rose and fell in turn. Each, at the height of their powers, looked unassailable, yet all rapidly collapsed one after another.

When we look at our current, globalised civilisation, we too are like the Roman citizen pointing to the wonders we have created. Despite the historical evidence to the contrary, we are convinced that our civilisation is going to last forever. In fact, we have more in common with the Roman citizen

---

[1] The British lost their first Empire in America in 1783, but went on to build an Asian, African and Middle Eastern Empire in the nineteenth century.

than our blindness to the simple fact that everything falls apart in the end. Beyond this, what unites us is that both of our civilisations depended upon an increasing supply of energy to grow. Once the energy available to us peaks, decline is inevitable.

Rome's energy was based on war and assimilation. Conquest provided the stored and embodied solar energy of the various peoples and provinces that were defeated and assimilated. Each conquest replenished the Roman treasury. But there was a sting in the tail. The boost from conquest was a once-and-for-good benefit. After a province had been plundered of its embodied energy, it fell back onto the energy (food) that it could produce from that year's harvest. Often, this meant that the cost of continuing to administer the assimilated province was higher than the income it generated. The only answer to this for a heavily armed empire was to conquer even more provinces. So conquest continued until the Roman Empire reached two kinds of limits. First, in Northwest Europe, it ran out of provinces that were worth plundering. Pict, Irish and German provinces offered no surplus, but still had to be defended against. Second, in the East it encountered enemies strong enough to present the prospect of defeat. Again, these provinces could not be plundered, but they had to be defended against. With further expansion blocked, and with insufficient energy to maintain the defence and administration of the Empire, was the result that it became prone to both revolts from within and incursions from without. Eventually the Empire shrank; slowly losing all of the Western Empire and ultimately losing the Byzantine Empire to the Turks.

Our Western Civilisation is also dependent upon energy for its growth. However, the energy that we deployed to grow was not (always) the accumulated surplus of neighbouring provinces. Ours was the concentrated store of millions of years of solar energy – fossil carbon (coal, oil and gas). These have provided us with a huge energy boost with which we have developed all of our technological wonders and with which we have expanded our economic system into every corner of the planet. But we have a similar predicament to the Romans – our energy too is a once-and-for-good benefit. It is a finite resource that cannot be replaced. And the geological evidence is that we are about halfway through it. That is to say, we are standing at the apex of our global civilisation. Three hundred years of fossil carbon-fuelled economic growth is about to come to an end *not* because we are about to run out of oil, but because we can no longer pump oil out of the ground in the quantities required to maintain adequate economic growth rates.

In this guide to the phenomenon of "Peak Oil" – the point at which we are producing *more* oil than we have ever done before… and more than we will ever do again – I set out the reasons why we now face a combination of dwindling oil supplies and increasing oil prices. This is not simply a matter of geology, as many of the detractors of peak oil believe. The economics of oil production and the geopolitics of supply play at least as important a role in our predicament as the geological and technological limits on future production.

The issues that I set out in this guide are very difficult psychologically. My own response as I researched this issue over the last five years was to go through the classic stages that we associate with bereavement – in my case the potential loss of a way of life that I had always taken for granted:

○ I experienced *shock* – why is nobody talking about these issues?

○ I experienced *denial* – the fact that nobody seems to be talking about this must mean that it is not really happening. Surely the few people that are talking about it must just be assorted cranks and conspiracy theorists

○ I experienced *fear* and *anger* over the loss of a way of life and the uncertainty about what comes after it

○ I began to *negotiate* – surely there will be a techno-logical fix. Surely clever people somewhere will come up with a solution

○ At times I felt *helpless* and *hopeless* – each new piece of news about the economy, the environment or the depletion of resources just seemed to make our predicament even more insurmountable

○ I often got *depressed* – unable to see how this could possibly turn out well

○ Sometimes I would feel *guilty* for not having done more about these issues when there was still time

○ Eventually I arrived at *acceptance* – we are where we are. Humans have been through worse. My own grandmother raised four children during the Second World War while her husband was away in the army. She would have known how to cope. And our generation can follow the example of her generation.

In reading this guide, you too may experience some of these emotions and responses. That is only natural. The story I am weaving together is about the vulnerability and lack of sustainability of our current civilisation. It is the story of a *predicament* rather than a problem; since a problem implies there is a solution. There is not – so we must hope that we are sufficiently resilient and adaptable to manage the change that is coming.

What follows is, in fact, just one element of the coming crisis of western civilisation. There are others, most notably the growing climate crisis together with the looming collapse of the global banking system which has now printed more than 400 percent more paper claims on wealth than there is wealth to claim. Sooner or later the massive private and public debt that the western world has run up since the 1980s is going to implode.

These are the "three E's" of our predicament – Energy, Economy, Environment. Underlying them is an even more intractable problem – population overshoot. There were just 3 billion people sharing the planet on the day I was born. In just 54 years, we have more than doubled, having just passed 7 billion. We are currently adding the equivalent of the population of Germany (around 80 million) every year. These are not just additional mouths to feed – a significant problem in its own right. They are also people who will grow up aspiring to a Western lifestyle. They will want to drive cars and live in central heated/air conditioned homes. They will expect to consume smart phones and computers, washing machines and refrigerators. As this population grows, and as these demands for improving lifestyles are met, our economy is forced to generate more and more energy and to pump more and more oil.

There is, however, a fly in this particular ointment – oil in particular and fossil carbon in general is a finite resource. It cannot be replenished, and we have reached the point at which we can no longer pump it out of the ground fast enough. Ten out of the last eleven economic crises – including the crash of 2008 – were immediately preceded and at least partially caused by a spike in oil prices. However, each time this has happened, oil production increased and prices fell allowing the economy to return to normal. This time it is different. This time there will be no *going back to normal.*

The Master Resource

Modern economics teaches us that all resources are infinitely substitutable provided that we get the price correct. If, for example, iron ore were to become rare, shortage would cause prices to rise. This, in turn, would drive up the price of steel, which would drive up the price of everything that uses steel in its manufacture. But there would come a point at which alternatives to steel would be cheaper. For example, many items that used to be made from steel are now made from carbon fibre. So, higher priced steel might result in a shift to carbon fibre that, ultimately, would overcome the shortage of steel and iron ore. Additionally, the higher price of steel is likely to trigger investment in science and technology both to find ways of extracting, recycling and reusing iron and steel more efficiently, and to develop alternatives to iron ore. According to modern economic theory, energy in general, and oil in particular, are just more infinitely substitutable resources. If one energy supply gets harder to obtain, the price will go up. This will make alternatives more affordable so companies will switch to the alternatives. Research and development funding will be used both to make the extraction of the energy resource more efficient, and to develop the alternatives. Wider society will barely notice the transition.

Unfortunately, modern economics are more akin to religion than to science. And just the fact that economists make such un-evidenced claims is no guarantee that they will bear any relationship to reality. Let us consider one very simple real world phenomenon – we do not drive solar powered cars. Battery powered cars today make up less than one percent of the global car fleet despite the fact that until recently oil prices had reached historically high levels in excess of $100 per barrel. Far from substitution, we continue to depend upon petroleum to drive our cars. There is good reason for this. Electric cars are more expensive and less effective. That is, while they are *a substitute* they are an *inferior* substitute for petroleum vehicles.

Paradoxically, one of the key reasons why electric cars are too expensive is that the price of oil has risen (the current temporary falls excepted) to historically high levels. Why? – because oil is *an essential ingredient,* not just in every component within the car itself but in the extraction and transportation of every mineral and metal involved in its manufacture. A standard car tyre alone requires seven barrels of oil to produce. The plastics involve tens of barrels. The extraction and transportation of the metals used in the manufacture of cars is highly oil dependent. This "embodied" oil may not be seen directly by the end user, but it is reflected in the price.

Another key barrier to the adoption of electric vehicles is the huge amount of energy and resources required to construct a suitable recharging/battery-replacement infrastructure similar to the network of filling stations for petroleum vehicles. Clearly, the creation of such an infrastructure will also be affected by the price of oil, so that the cost will rise just at the point where the need for substitution is growing – the opposite of what economists believe should happen.

Nor is the reason we do not drive electric cars for want of technology. We have the ability to build electric cars that perform as well as many of the petrol and diesel cars that we used to drive just a few decades ago. There are problems with range because of the limits of battery technology, although given that most journeys are less than five miles this is by no means a deal breaker. Indeed, for most drivers most of the time the experience of driving an electric car would be no different to driving a petrol or diesel car – save that they would be preventing tons of additional carbon dioxide being burned into the atmosphere. The real barrier to adoption of this technology – once we follow the supply chains back far enough – is the shortage, and therefore increased price – of the oil that electric cars are supposed to wean us off!

Humanity has a blind spot when we examine our use of oil. Because we see petroleum going into our cars or (for a minority) our heating systems, we assume this is the only point at which we consume oil. We tend to be less aware of our collective consumption of the oil used to transport all of the goods that we buy. We are particularly unaware of the amount of oil that we consume when we take a flight. However, even when we add up all of the oil consumed in all of these direct forms of transportation, these account for just half of our total oil consumption. The other half of our oil consumption is hidden – embodied in all of the component parts of just about everything we rely upon and consume. From the food we eat to the phones we communicate with, the computers we work on and the homes we live in, all required massive quantities of oil in extraction and manufacture. Oil is used in pharmaceuticals, pesticides and herbicides, fertilisers, toothpaste and tooth brushes, packaging, plastics, food processing and food packaging, furniture manufacture, double glazing, pharmaceuticals; the list goes on. There is barely a product in your home or your place of work that did not require oil in its manufacture. Indeed, the average European consumes around a tonne of oil every year:

> "In Germany, approximately 100 million tonnes of oil are consumed per year. This corresponds to more than one tonne per inhabitant, approximately 500 oil tankers, or a cube with an edge length of approximately 480 metres."[2]

Only half of Germany's oil consumption is in transport. The remainder is embodied oil used to manufacture goods.

This raises the question of whether oil is substitutable. Theoretically it is. During the Second World War, Germany depended upon synthetic oil (made from coal) to continue fighting once the Romanian oilfields had been overrun by the Red Army in 1944. But coal is considerably less energy dense than oil. Whereas a kilogramme of coal contains 27

---

[2] Bundeswehr Transformation Centre. November 2010. *Armed Forces, Capabilities and Technologies in the 21st Century Environmental Dimensions of Security.* Sub-study 1 - PEAK OIL: Security policy implications of scarce resources. P12

mega joules of energy, a kilogramme of oil contains 45 mega joules. So using coal to make synthetic oil actually costs energy – but without oil, it is impossible to fight a mechanised war.

Today we can make liquid biofuels as a substitute for oil. We do this most efficiently in Brazil where sugar cane is used; we do it much less efficiently in the USA where corn is used. Corn-based ethanol costs more energy to produce than it provides in return, and is only economical with huge government subsidies.

Scientists are currently developing algae-based biofuels that are chemically identical to oil, and which do not require agricultural land for production. It is not clear whether these can be produced without losing energy in the process. There are also questions about whether algae-based biofuels can be scaled-up sufficiently to replace declining conventional oil production.

Other forms of so-called "tight oil" or "unconventional oil" are also being added to the mix. In Canada too, high oil prices allowed the development of massive tar sand production. These fuels can all substitute for conventional oil... but at what cost to the economy? One of the reasons for the current fall in the global oil price is that the USA has successfully extracted millions of barrels of oil by hydraulically fracturing its massive shale deposits, but consumers cannot afford to buy this oil at the high prices needed to produce it.

There are no renewable energy substitutes for oil. The most common renewables – solar, wind, hydroelectric and tidal – are substitutes for coal and gas. That is, they will generate cleaner electricity that can be supplied to households and businesses via the National Grid. However, they cannot currently be converted into viable liquid fuels. Hydrogen *might* emerge to meet this need. There are already working hydrogen vehicles. For example, in Iceland, buses run on hydrogen while in the USA the main car manufacturers have working prototypes for demonstration purposes. However, hydrogen should be viewed as a form of energy storage rather than a fuel. Hydrogen does not normally occur in nature other than as a part of a compound – most commonly bound together with oxygen in water. At present, most hydrogen is produced from natural (i.e. methane) gas – the prices of which are rising almost as rapidly as the price of oil. To manufacture hydrogen by electrolysing water would involve a huge electricity input from renewables or nuclear, and would most probably make it too expensive as an alternative to petroleum.

We have a problem with oil that current economic thinking does not acknowledge. Oil is not just another $100 resource that can be substituted at will. Oil has quite rightly been called "the master resource". This is not simply because it is embodied in everything we use. It is also because of the huge power that it has bestowed upon our civilisation. Energy expert Richard Heinberg[3] explains this by asking us to consider how much effort it takes just to push a car to the side of the road if it has broken down. Just a few yards of pushing are a hard slog. Now imagine you had to push the same car for thirty miles. How long would that take you? Perhaps a month of back-breaking hard labour, depending on how fit you are. A gallon of petrol will push the same car the same 30 miles, up and down hills, in just half an hour. That is an example of the power that oil has bestowed upon us.

The 80-90 million barrels a day of oil that humanity consumes provides us, in effect, with trillions of uncomplaining oil slaves doing work that would otherwise have to be done by animals and humans, or that simply would not get done at all. Nat Hagens[4] calculates the human labour equivalent of a single barrel of oil (159 litres) at 11 years. That is, for less than $100 we get the equivalent of 11 "labourers" working for us for a year. At the UK minimum wage, this would cost us £153,296 and at the average wage, £277,420 – that's a lot of work for just £63 ($100)!

From the turn of the twentieth century we have added a massive quantity of oil to our global energy mix. More recently, we have added smaller amounts of natural gas and nuclear. And we still consume large volumes of coal, wood

[3] www.postcarbon.org/our-people/richard-heinberg
[4] www.themonkeytrap.us

and peat. However, it is oil that gives us the biggest energy
bang for our buck. And this leaves us vulnerable to any drop
in production, as this cannot be automatically addressed by
ramping up the production of alternative sources of energy.

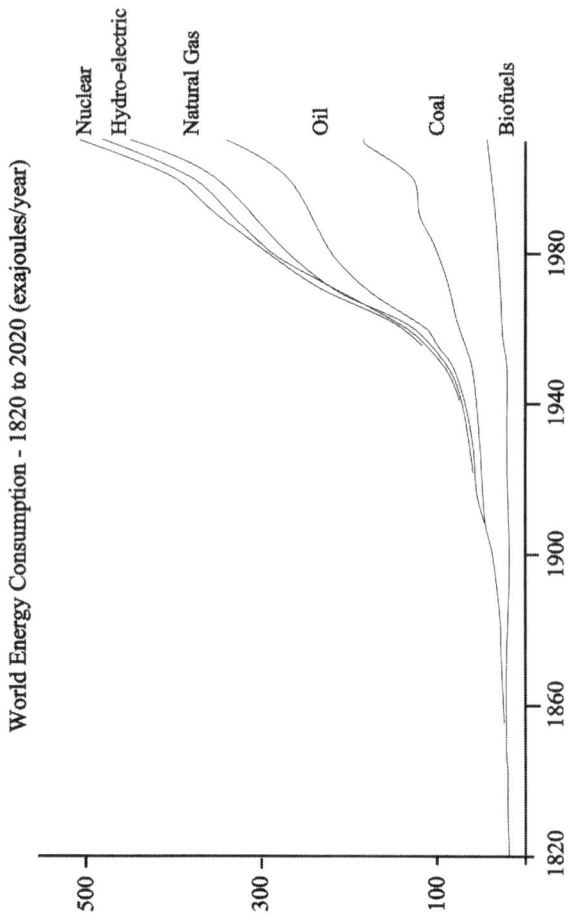

World Energy Consumption - 1820 to 2020 (exajoules/year)

Half Way Through

The oil that we consume today began to be formed between 80 and 300 million years ago. Trillions and trillions of tiny plants called phytoplankton lived in shallow, warm seas covering areas such as those that today correspond to Saudi Arabia, the Caspian Basin, the North Sea and Texas/Gulf of Mexico. These tiny plants were able to grow to a much greater number than their environment could sustain. As a result, they sucked oxygen out of the water, replacing it with noxious sulphur dioxide, creating vast dead zones below the surface of the seas. This resulted in the deaths of the phytoplankton themselves, together with any fish and plants that happened to stray into the dead zones. These life forms – and, crucially, the embodied solar energy they contained – sank to the sea bed where they formed layer upon layer of sticky black oozing mud.

Over time the Earth's tectonic plates moved, causing the shallow sea beds to sink beneath continental rock formations. Under pressure from the rocks above and heated from the Earth's mantle below, over millions of years the oozing black mud was "cooked" into oil. (Where it was over-cooked, it became natural gas. Where it was under-cooked, it remained as oil shale). Most of the oil that was formed by this process simply seeped to the surface and evaporated. But in some areas, the oil was trapped beneath a cap of impermeable rock, and formed into reservoirs. The biggest of these became the Ghawar oil field in Saudi Arabia.

Oil had been known about for centuries. The Ancient Chinese used oil in lamps, while the Ancient Greeks used it to make "Greek Fire" – an early flame-thrower weapon. However, since only that oil that rose to the surface could be used, there was never sufficient to develop an industry. Moreover, since few societies had use for it, oil was more often regarded as a nuisance, poisoning water courses and killing livestock.

In the mid-nineteenth century, armed with a greater understanding of chemistry, entrepreneurs began wondering whether oil might offer an alternative to whale oil as a lighting fuel and a lubricant. The ability to refine kerosene from crude oil at a time when whale stocks were declining drove the first oil prospecting in the USA. Initially, prospectors searched in those areas – like Pennsylvania – where oil was already known to seep from the ground. In practice, this meant that the first oil wells only required around 70 feet of drilling in order to tap into the oil reservoirs. Initially, the Pennsylvania oil boom was based on the sale of kerosene for lighting. However, it was two of the waste products from refining kerosene – a gas called petrol (gasoline) and a liquid called diesel – that were to drive the oil industry in the twentieth century. The development of the internal combustion engine after 1860 paved the way for the motorised civilisation of the modern world. Nowhere else was this more true than in the USA, where all of the resources and skills needed to develop an automobile industry were present, and where a growing, affluent population was to provide the mass market.

Prior to the Second World War, the USA emerged as by far the biggest oil producer on the planet, eclipsing the Soviet Union's Caucasus, and the British Empire's Persian oil fields. Indeed, perhaps the single key reason why the allies won the Second World War was the sheer volume of oil – and the industrial capacity that this gave rise to – that (especially in the USA) they had access to.

Following the war, everything looked rosy. Not only did the USA have massive oil production of its own, but it had also negotiated a deal with Saudi Arabia to ensure that the vast reserves of oil in that country would be developed by US oil companies and would be traded internationally in Dollars. There was, however, a fly in the ointment. In 1956, M. King Hubbert, a geologist working for the Shell oil company published research suggesting that US oil production would peak around 40 years after its oil discoveries had peaked. Since US oil discoveries had peaked in 1930, Hubbert proposed that peak production would come sometime around 1970.

Hubbert's research was ridiculed at the time. And in 1970, when journalists began to run stories about how this was meant to be the peak year for US oil production, industry insiders laughed once more, pointing out that the US oil fields were producing more oil than they ever had done. It turned out that in 1970, the US oil fields were also producing more oil than they ever would again. Hubbert was correct. Oil production had peaked. An oil-thirsty USA found itself increasingly dependent upon imported oil, especially from the Middle East. Sensing this new US weakness, the oil producing (OPEC) countries – led by Saudi Arabia – saw their chance to improve their income from oil exports, and in 1973 turned off the taps. The resulting oil shortages in the USA and Europe gave a taste of what might happen to an economy that has been built around cheap and easy access to oil. Together with concern about future access to a range of resources set out in The Club of Rome's *Limits to Growth* computer simulation[5] that suggested an end to economic growth in the first decades of the twenty-first century, the oil shocks led, briefly, to government initiatives to wean the economy off oil.

Standard Hubbert Curve

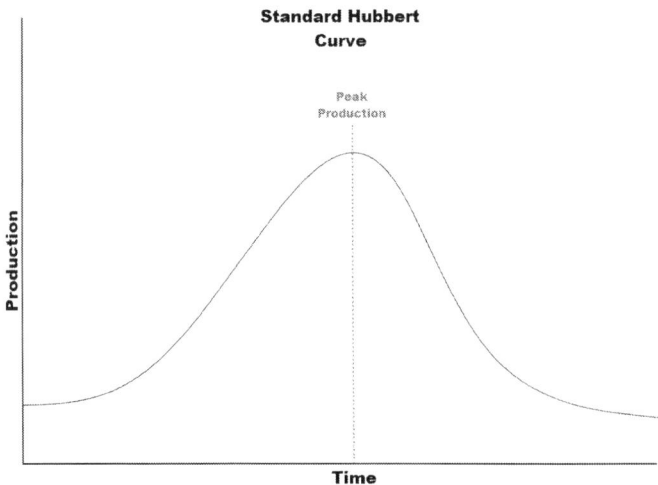

[5] Meadows, D.H., Meadows, D.L., Randers J. and Behrens III W.W. 1972. *The Limits to Growth: a report for the club of Rome's project on the predicament of mankind.* Universe Books.

However, in part, Hubbert was wrong. As a geologist, Hubbert was only looking at the amounts of oil in the various US oil fields. He reasoned that "peak oil" would occur when the half-way point was reached. That is, when we reached the point where we had extracted half of the available oil. So the productive life of an oil field would appear like a bell curve.

It would also be possible to amalgamate all of the data for all of the oil fields in a given country in order to arrive at a similar bell curve that would show the point at which that country's oil production would peak. Of course, if you can do this for any one country, it is also possible to do it for *all* countries.

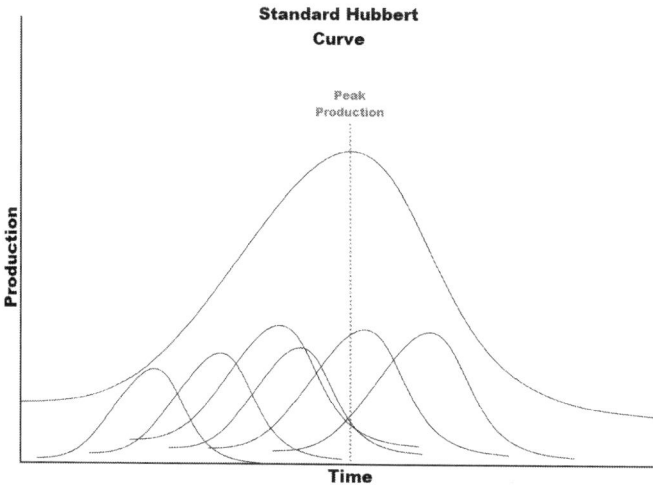

Standard Hubbert Curve

Peak Production

Production

Time

Based on the fact that the peak of oil discovery came in 1964 – we continue to find oil, but the fields are much smaller, suggesting that we have, indeed, already found all of the best oil reserves – Hubbert had predicted that the peak of world oil production would come in 2004. Once again, oil industry insiders laughed at the theory because, in 2004 the world was producing more oil than it had ever done. Then, in 2005, world production of *conventional* crude oil peaked, and has continued to fall to this day.

Once again, Hubbert's basic reasoning had been proved correct; and with dramatic consequences – there is little doubt that the resulting oil price spike in 2006 was the trigger point for the global financial crash of 2008 and the ensuing depression that continues to stifle the global economy. Because oil is the master resource, the price spike quickly fed through into increasing prices, particularly in the USA. In an attempt to stave off this inflation, the US central bank (followed by central banks around the world) raised interest rates. However, higher interest rates left thousands of sub-prime mortgage holders unable to service their debts, causing defaults and bankruptcies. Banks around the world found themselves holding "assets" that were worthless. The rest is history.

Hubbert was correct about the geology of oil. There is, broadly, a halfway point along the bell curve of oil extraction at which production peaks. However, Hubbert failed to factor ecology, engineering and economics into his models. As a result, his simple bell curve does not fully describe what happens when global production peaks. Hubbert's US model proved correct only because the US oil fields were just a part of a wider global oil industry which still had plenty of cheap and easy reserves to be exploited. As a result, it was more profitable to invest in drilling new oil fields – such as those in the North Sea – than to attempt the kind of technical developments that would be needed to boost production in fields that were already past their peak. It was easier – and still profitable – to simply allow these older fields to deplete. So a simple bell curve more or less described what happened.

At a global scale, however, with many more countries past their peak, and far too few easy oilfields left to develop, the economics are different. As oil has become harder to obtain, prices have risen. This has created a situation in which investing in both unconventional oil and boosting production from already depleting fields has become viable. Where this is done, the production curve is different.

After the initial, gradual decline in production, efforts are made to boost extraction once more, and new *unconventional* sources of oil (shale, tar sands, deep water and Arctic) are added to the mix, leading to a "fat tail". However, as there is no more newly discovered oil, we are simply extracting what is left at a faster rate, meaning that ultimately, production falls off a sharp cliff. This effect includes the current fracking (hydraulic fracturing) boom. The shale oil deposits that are currently being exploited, and those (such as in the UK) where the oil industry has plans to frack, are

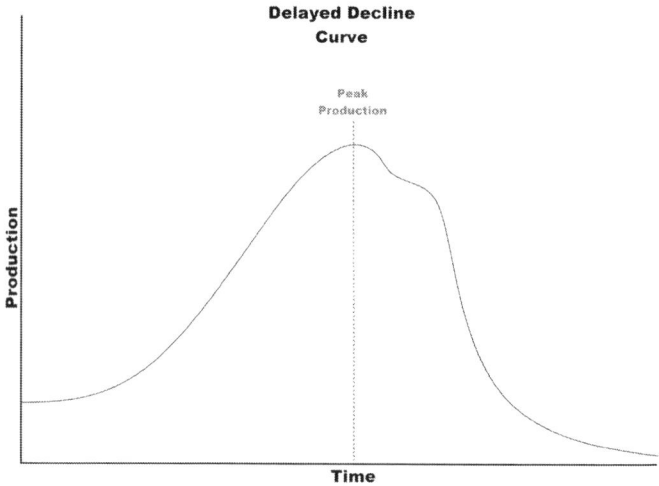

Delayed Decline Curve

Peak Production

Production

Time

not new discoveries – they have been known about for decades. They are being exploited today solely because cheap and easy oil fields are depleting and the resulting high prices make fracking economically viable. But shale oil is very different to crude oil. Shale oil formations are essentially rocks containing deposits of oil that did not complete the process either of rising to the surface and evaporating, or (more usefully) forming into reservoirs that could be drilled. The hydraulic fracturing process is an expensive and technically difficult way of artificially completing the process.

Fracking involves releasing and concentrating much smaller amounts of liquid oil than would be found in a conventional oil field. The consequence of this is that the life of a fracking well is incredibly short – on average, production falls by

80-90 percent in three years. So, the only way in which production can be maintained is by drilling thousands of new wells across a massive area – something that bodes ill for those intending to frack in the UK. Even prior to the fall in oil prices that has rendered the fracking industry unprofitable, a growing body of scientists and economists had reached the view that the fracking boom is actually a bubble, and that industry claims that the boom would last into the 2040s are about 20 years too optimistic.

One thing that is certain is that even if the most optimistic forecasts for unconventional oil are true, they are still not sufficient to allow continued energy growth (and therefore economic growth). The best they can offer is to put the problem off for a few more years. To carry on with business as usual, we need to discover the equivalent of five new Saudi Arabias. But the geology is working against us. Our discoveries of oil peaked in 1964. What oil there is still waiting to be discovered will be in much smaller deposits and will require much greater investments (at much higher prices) to extract and transport. Whatever else unfolds in future, the one thing we can be confident about is that the days of cheap oil – and therefore cheap energy – are at an end.

Optimal Foraging Theory

The difficulties besetting the fracking industry in the face of falling global oil prices are a proxy for a less well known but much more worrying peak oil issue – "net energy" or "energy return on energy investment" (EROI).

Biologists and ecologists have long understood this concept, but it is one that economics has long since forgotten. In nature, nothing happens without energy; and it takes energy to obtain energy. So we have food chains that begin with plants converting solar energy into sugars and starches. These are consumed by herbivores (plant-eating animals at the base of the food chain), which are, in turn, preyed upon by carnivores (the meat-eating animals higher up the food chain). Along the food chain, each plant and animal has to find an efficient ratio of energy expended for energy obtained. Biologists refer to this as "optimal foraging theory". The idea is that each evolves so that it expends an optimal amount of energy in order to obtain not only the energy required to maintain its own existence, but also the energy required to reproduce. So, for example, a peacock must eat enough insects to keep itself alive *and* to grow an ornate plumage sufficient to attract a peahen mate with which to breed and rear young. A cheetah will expend a large amount of energy in an extraordinary burst of speed in order to catch and eat a gazelle, because this will provide sufficient energy to keep her alive and to feed her young. However, it would be energy-inefficient for the cheetah to attempt to consume either a zebra or a mouse – the former would take too much energy to consume, while the latter would provide too little energy to be worthwhile.

Humans are bound by the same energy constraints, but we have been inventive in finding ways of pushing back the boundaries. Starting with the social advantage enjoyed by many mammals, we were able to cooperate in order to deploy our collective energy to good effect. Our hunting and gathering ancestors were able to kill and eat much larger and more powerful animals than would have been possible had they operated as lone individuals. The same is true for their ability to harvest and prepare grains, fruits and vegetables. Use of fire allowed our ancestors to cook foods that would otherwise have needed to be chewed and digested for much longer periods – requiring more of their limited energy. Over time, this allowed their teeth and digestive systems to become smaller, while their brains were able to grow larger and their hands more dextrous. Fire also provided them with heat, allowing them to extend their range beyond Africa.

Our hunting and gathering ancestors generated sufficient *surplus* energy to enable a basic division of labour, allowing some members of the group to specialise in such things as tool making and tanning, which, in turn, allowed them to obtain even more energy. However, it was the development of agriculture that provided the first big energy break for humans. Agriculture generated so much additional energy (nearly 700 percent of the energy produced by hunter-gatherers[7]) that it enabled the development of the first

[7] See for example, Mahli, Y. 2014. "The Metabolism of the Human Dominated Planet" in Goldin, I. (ed) *The Planet is Full*. Oxford University Press.

civilisations – urban populations that depended upon imported food for their continued survival. Often, these early civilisations would fall foul of periodic famines, floods and droughts that would suddenly and catastrophically reduce their energy supply, leading to collapse. But where they survived, they often developed the means and the opportunity to use force to obtain energy supplies.

Once groups of humans had sufficient surplus food (i.e. energy), neighbouring groups had a motive to use force to steal the surplus. Those civilisations that were strong enough and skilled enough could develop stealing into rudimentary warfare, using their surplus energy to create and deploy specialist soldiers and sailors to raid and conquer neighbouring groups and provinces. This paved the way for the major civilisations of the ancient world – the Egyptians, Assyrians, Greeks, and, later the Romans.

These early civilisations faced a particularly pressing energy problem: they were obliged to survive largely on the energy provided directly by the sun. That is, with the exception of some wood burning, wind and water power, their energy came from the crops and livestock that their land area could provide. One obvious – but short-term – solution to this constraint was to conquer neighbouring peoples. This allowed them to obtain the *embodied* solar energy of these societies. That is, they obtained all of the wealth that the neighbouring civilisation has accumulated to that date. However, this kind of accumulation is ultimately counterproductive since, once the wealth had been consumed, the – now larger – empire had to fall back upon immediate solar energy once more. For the Roman Empire, this round of conquest continued until the Empire came up against on the one hand Celtic and German neighbours too poor to be worth conquering, and on the other hand a Persian neighbour militarily equal to themselves. Once these limits were reached, declining energy led to the gradual but remorseless decline of the Empire itself.

It is worth noting that the divisions of labour that develop in energy-rich human societies, while having superficial differences, are in fact very similar. This is true even where civilisations have evolved without contact with other human civilisations, suggesting that all human societies develop divisions of labour best suited to optimising energy use:

> "What took place in the early 1500s was truly exceptional, something that had never happened before and never will again. Two cultural experiments, running in isolation for 15,000 years or more, at last came face to face. Amazingly, after all that time, each could recognise the other's institutions. When Cortes landed in Mexico he found roads, canals, cities, palaces, schools, law courts, markets, irrigation works, kings, priests, temples, peasants, artisans, armies, astronomers, merchants, sports, theatre, art, music, and books. High civilisation, differing in detail but alike in essentials, had evolved independently on both sides of the earth."[8]

[8] Wright, R. 2004. *A Short History of Progress*. pp50-51.

What makes us different in the modern world has nothing to do with intelligence or biological evolution. Indeed, were it possible to go back in time and bring a Stone Age baby into the present, it would grow up in exactly the same way and with the same abilities as a twenty-first century child. The *only* thing that really separates us from them is the once-and-for-good gift of fossil carbon.

When Britain began to industrialise from the mid-eighteenth century, it contained as much fossil carbon in the form of coal as Saudi Arabia contained in oil. Coupled to abundant iron, copper and tin deposits, and tied into a growing maritime economy, this gave Britain a huge advantage over its neighbours. In the course of the following century, Britain created the largest empire (in both population and land mass) the world has ever known. More importantly, Britain exported its model of credit-based capitalism – later developed by the USA – around the world.

Economists such as Adam Smith, looking at a fast industrialising Britain, convinced themselves that it was *trade* that was the key to the wealth of nations. In particular, free – i.e. unregulated and without barriers – trade was the means by which all nations would be enriched. Indeed, to this day the leaders of the western world persist in trying to export their model of free trade to countries whose development is patently stunted by it. One reason for this is that the classical economists were fundamentally wrong about the wealth of nations.

The thing that made Britain "great" in the eighteenth and nineteenth century was that vast reserve of coal which provided the equivalent of millions of uncomplaining energy slaves that could be harnessed to drive the blast furnaces, factories, the ships and the railways around which a modern industrial economy was built. Vast reserves of coal beneath Germany and the USA allowed those two countries to surpass Britain by the end of the nineteenth century, by which time an even more powerful and versatile fossil carbon – oil – was emerging to eclipse coal. In the final analysis, oil was the deciding factor in which of Germany and the USA would emerge as the dominant power, taking over the mantle of the rapidly declining British Empire. While the USA was blessed with massive reserves of oil, allowing the development of an oil-based industrial economy, Germany depended upon coal and was forced to spend precious foreign reserves to import oil from neighbouring countries. In the Second World War – which, after December 10th 1941 became a war between the USA and the USSR on one side and Germany on the other, Germany's two campaigns – in the Caucasus and (to a lesser degree) North Africa were aimed at securing oil. When they failed, Germany was doomed. Indeed, it is instructive that when the USA invaded Northwest France in 1944, every one of its divisions was motorised, whereas eighty-five percent of the German divisions depended upon horse-drawn transport.

Fossil carbon is the energy source that separates our civilisation from all previous ones. All previous civilisations were obliged to exist on immediate solar energy for all but a fraction of their activities. Most of the day-to-day work of these earlier economies was powered by food – either the fodder provided to work animals or the food consumed by humans. Those societies that were able to harness wind and water power were able to gain a competitive advantage – for example, developing large ocean-going sailing ships that opened up colonisation and world trade. However, even these advantages were at the mercy of the seasons – ships could easily get stuck in the Doldrums for weeks at a time, while others would be torn apart when they were hit by hurricane force winds. Drought would remove water power as well as setting the scene for poor harvests and famine.

Fossil carbon gradually allowed us to transcend this dependence upon the vagaries of our environment – it is a key reason why we tend to view ourselves as in some way living *outside* or *beyond* nature today. Steam power rapidly replaced humans, animals, water and wind as the energy behind our manufacturing and transportation. Steam-driven production lines were not subject to interruption from droughts and floods in the way water-powered factories had been. Steam ships did not have to wait for the wind in order to set out across the oceans. Steam locomotives allowed for faster transportation across continents than for sailing around them – reversing conditions that had prevailed for more than 500 years, and allowing continental powers such as the USA and Russia to emerge as major economies.

The internal combustion engine took our civilisation to exalted heights. The automobile revolutionised cities, allowing a massive, car-dependent suburban population to grow outside the commercial and industrial districts of the old city centres. Agriculture was transformed as petroleum-powered machinery took the place of working animals, and reduced the need for farm workers. The quality of people's diets improved as a new petroleum-powered transport network allowed a greater variety of foods to be transported from further afield into the developing towns and cities.

All of these trends have expanded to the global scale today. We think nothing, for example, of eating Chilean strawberries in December – taking for granted a transportation system that allows these fruits to be picked, packaged, transported by truck to an airport, then flown to the UK and transported to a supermarket within a matter of hours. Much of our clothing is shipped in from Asia, while our smartphones and computers are manufactured in gargantuan Chinese factories employing up to a quarter of a million workers. The materials from which our electronic equipment is made are themselves shipped from around the world into China for manufacture. And all of this happens on a "just-in-time" basis.

Take away fossil carbon in general, and oil in particular, and none of this would have been possible. Without fossil carbon, the best we might have achieved would have been an approximation of the fifteenth century Spanish and Portuguese Empires, or perhaps the sixteenth century Dutch

Empire. However, vastly more of our energy would have been tied to agriculture as people would have been obliged to produce food for themselves and their animals, and to produce enough of a surplus to maintain the division of labour.

In geological terms, of course, there is absolutely no chance of us running out of oil, coal or gas. However, it is the *economic* reason why we will never run out that is a cause for very real concern. A cheetah will run down a very young, very old or infirm gazelle in preference to taking on a fit adult. This is because the energy (or cost) to the cheetah is much less when it hunts these "low-hanging fruit" than when it takes on more difficult prey. In the same way, we have harvested fossil carbon on a low-hanging fruit first basis. The first coal used by humans was on the surface. Only later did we dig mines; and only when these were exhausted did we go into deep mining and under-sea mining. Today, we use explosives to blast the tops off mountains and – with the help of massive petroleum-powered digging and hauling machines – dig down miles into the ground beneath to secure supplies of coal (and many minerals). We would not be doing this were there still abundant coal supplies just below the surface. The development of the oil industry is similar. The first wells were drilled in regions where oil seeped to the surface. When these were exhausted, we moved on to deeper land-based drilling. As these early oil fields peaked, we introduced new technologies and techniques – at a cost – to keep production up. These additional costs made less easy oil fields – such as those beneath the North Sea –

profitable to develop. Today, after the global peak of conventional crude oil, it has become profitable[9] to develop unconventional oil – Arctic, very deep water, oil shale (i.e. fracking) and tar sands – which requires massively more investment in comparison to conventional oil.

While we experience this situation in terms of price increases (and temporary falls when demand drops), we are in a similar position to a cheetah that has successfully hunted down all of the young, old and infirm gazelle and is now obliged to expend much more energy hunting down (and more often failing to kill) the fit adults. That is, we have to deploy more of our energy reserves to get the same energy back. And just as a cheetah in this position finds that its ability to breed and to rear young is put under pressure by this energy constraint, so our ability to operate a complex global economy is pressurised as we have to divert an increasing proportion of our energy and resources to securing our future energy needs.

Were a cheetah (or any other animal) to reach a point where it would need to expend more energy than it gets in return,

[9] Current low prices suggest that when prices are high enough to make unconventional oil profitable, the dampening effect on global demand is so strong as to rapidly reduce demand. One by-product of the 2014/15 price fall has been a massive capital flight away from further development of unconventional oil. When global demand picks up once more, it is likely that we will rapidly experience supply problems leading to large price increases once more.

it would not move. It would sit and conserve energy until either some easier prey came by or it starved. In the global economy, we tend to use the price mechanism to the same end. Any human economic activity that delivers less than it costs is considered unprofitable. It either adapts to become profitable or it is abandoned. Behind the price mechanism is the expenditure of energy – human labour, externally generated energy, the energy embodied in all of the resources required for production, and the embodied energy in the capital deployed.   When the economic activity is the extraction of fossil carbon (or, indeed, the construction of renewables) for energy generation or transportation, it is essential that the energy returned is higher than the energy invested. It would make no sense to invest a barrel of oil just to obtain the energy equivalent of a barrel of oil – we would be better off just using the barrel we already had. As Charles A.S. Hall[10] has pointed out, at an *energy return on investment* (EROI) of 1:1, all we get to do is *look at* the oil we get out of the ground. If we want to transport it to a refinery and convert it into petroleum products for human use, we need an EROI close to 3:1. This leaves us in an unpleasant predicament because oil shale and tar sands have an EROI of somewhere between at best 5:1 and at worst 1.5:1, while corn ethanol – currently our only renewable alternative transport fuel – has an EROI below 1:1; something only achievable in the USA because of huge

[10] Hall, Charles A.S. and Klitgaard, Kent A. 2012. *Energy and the Wealth of Nations: Understanding the Biophysical Economy.* Springer.

government subsidies. Similarly low EROI ratios apply to most of the renewable energy technologies. For example, photovoltaic solar panels give an EROI of around 5:1.

This raises a very serious question – just how much *net* energy does our complex global economy require in order to maintain economic growth rates of at least 2 percent (below which we tend to experience crises, recessions and depressions)? Perhaps more pertinently, what will the UK economy look like if the replacements for North Sea oil and gas can only manage an EROI of somewhere between 5:1 and 10:1?

Discretionary and Non-Discretionary Energy

Most economists see the economy as an interaction between firms (which produce goods and services) and households (which consume goods and services). These households also provide the capital and labour required by firms:

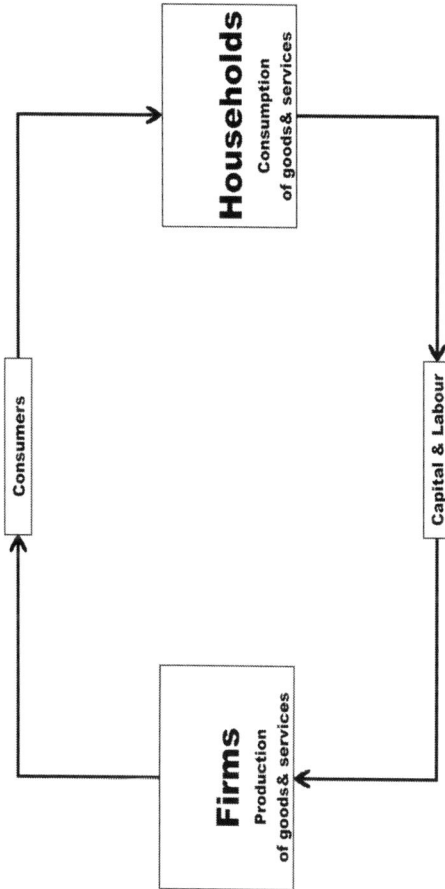

The raw materials and energy needed for production are often ignored (as are the heat and pollution generated). Where they are not, they are simply assumed to always be available in the desired quantities (and therefore not worth worrying about). This is because economists assume that the free market system will always generate adequate supplies through the price mechanism. That is, if there is a temporary shortage of a raw material, demand will push the price up. As the price of the raw material rises, it will become profitable to obtain new (perhaps more expensive to obtain) sources or to deploy new technologies to recycle. As the new and recycled resource(s) are exploited, technical efficiencies will lower and ultimately stabilise the price once more.

In this model, energy is treated as just another resource. If the price of an energy source (for example, oil) increases, it becomes viable to obtain new – more expensive – sources (for example, shale plays and tar sands). It is assumed that as these new sources are exploited, so prices will fall, thereby returning the system to equilibrium. However, while mineral resources can be recycled and natural resources can be replenished, fossil carbon is a once-and-for-good resource that follows the second law of thermodynamics – that is, broadly, in the process of using energy to produce work, we transform energy into dissipated heat which cannot be used in future. This means that while the price of most resources falls over time, the price of fossil carbon reaches a limit beyond which shortage drives prices upward.

Economists assume no limits to this economic system even though scientists from a range of disciplines are unequivocal about the finite supplies of fossil carbon and raw materials on Earth. Technical efficiency may bring prices down in the short-term, but this can only be at the expense of consuming a finite resource at an even faster rate than we had been previously. As such, demand is bound to overtake supply relatively quickly, resulting in an even bigger hike in prices later on.

Unlike economists, engineers view the economy as something that exists within a wider system of energy and resource exploitation. In this system, the economy can only exist provided it can be supplied with sufficient energy and natural resources. It must also be able to manage the excess heat, pollution and environmental damage that result from the production and consumption processes.

Without energy there is no production. Without natural resources there is no production. Without production there can be no consumption. And without a permanent cycle of production and consumption there can be no global economy. However, even this more complex model does not fully describe what is going on:

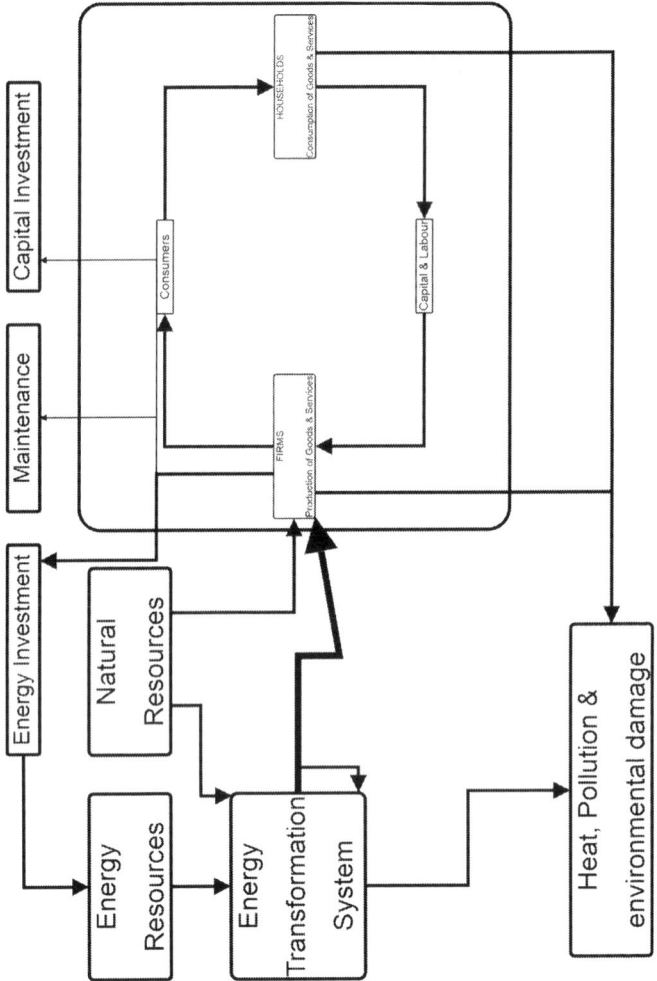

In addition to securing future fossil carbon, we must set energy and resources aside to maintain the system we currently have. We must educate and train the next generation of engineers and technicians required to operate the system. We have to invest in research and development in order to find new and efficient means of operating the system in future. All of this comes at a cost.

One way of looking at this is to divide the sum of the capital, labour, energy and resources available to us into *discretionary* and *non-discretionary* spending. We understand this within our households – there are things (mortgage payments, food, water, fuel, etc.) that we have little choice but to pay. There are other things (meals out, cinema, extra phone minutes, etc.) that we can choose, but are not obliged to purchase. The same is true for society as a whole. There are things that we have no choice but to pay for – food production, clean water, energy – and things that we can exercise choice over – healthcare, pensions, public services, business activities. The problem with energy is that it is the most non-discretionary of all. No energy = no civilisation. It is that simple.

Another way of looking at a falling EROI ratio is that the amount of discretionary energy available to society is falling. That is, we have to divert an increasing proportion of our total energy to maintaining the essential infrastructure, educating and training the engineers, researching and developing future technology and, crucially, extracting future fossil carbon and/or building and installing renewables. In practice, this leaves us with less energy (and labour, capital and resources) for discretionary use. We experience this process not as an energy shortage but as a price signal – the price of energy increases, crowding out our discretionary spending:

> "One vicious cycle playing out in America starts with the consumer, who has had to cut back on energy use. Less energy translates into less mobility, less shopping, and in general fewer consumer expenditures. Fewer consumer expenditures mean less demand and more pressure on corporations, which are also squeezed by higher resource costs. Wages in turn get squeezed, but resource prices remain high, and the vicious circle is completed. It is no surprise that this century has seen a 10% decline in real median income, which when measured in time and depth is probably the most protracted on record."[11]

Actually, the economic feedback to high energy prices occurs both at the bottom *and the top* of the income scale. Where the poor cut back, the rich go "off-grid". As the cost of micro-scale renewable energy generation (solar, wind,

[11] Stephen Leeb. 6.5.13. *Dangerous Times As Energy Sources Get Costlier To Extract.* Forbes.
http://www.forbes.com/sites/greatspeculations/2013/06/05/dangerous-times-as-energy-sources-get-costlier-to-extract/

geothermal, etc) has fallen, so thousands of (mainly affluent) households have begun to generate their own electricity *and* sell any excess back to the Grid. However, for the time being, this activity is essentially parasitic. Since it is impossible to live entirely off grid, these affluent households remain reliant on the Grid for those periods when they cannot generate enough energy. However, they are no longer contributing to the maintenance of the Grid that they depend upon.

This raises what should be a key political issue – how do we fund the Grid in future? At present, the electricity grid is funded through capital expenditure from the generating companies. This investment is possible only because those companies can promise investors that they will generate sufficient future profits to pay a return on the investment. If, however, an increasing number of households at the bottom of the income scale are "voluntarily" disconnecting themselves, and a large number at the top are being paid to go off grid, the only means of maintaining profit rates is to further squeeze those households in the middle. Obviously, this only serves to push even more households out at the bottom, while encouraging even more at the top to go off grid. Ultimately, the energy companies cannot remain profitable. Investors will flee. Maintenance will fail. Our energy supply will become intermittent.

Consider how easy it will be in future to operate a complex global economy, dependent upon highly integrated just-in-time supply chains, if our electricity supply becomes (probably randomly) intermittent. For many modern business activities, this is barely better than having no electricity at all. Supplies can no longer be relied on. Banking becomes difficult. There will be periods where operations have to shut down, but employees still have to be paid.

The operation of electricity grids is perhaps the easiest example of how a falling EROI can have a serious impact on the operation of critical infrastructure. However, we tend not to see the global transportation system in the same way. This is because the system is superficially more pluralistic. Whereas there is only one grid, sewage and water system, communications network and bank transfer system, transport consists of a network of infrastructure and facilities – ports, railways, roads, airports, etc – that are utilised by millions of vehicles – planes, ships, trains, trucks and cars – operated by thousands of companies. Nevertheless, the transportation system depends on volume use in the same way as the grid. It is rare for a company to operate its own private transportation. Usually even the biggest global corporations depend upon the availability of space on other companies' vehicles. Even a big global corporation like Amazon will use third-party carriers to transport goods from its warehouses to its consumers. The same is true on the supply side of the main food retailers. Each depends upon transport companies to be profitable in order to continue moving essential food stocks into and across the country. For the transport companies to remain profitable they depend upon full loads in order to keep prices competitive.

Increasing fuel prices undermine the system. As with the Grid example, the risk is that customers drop off the bottom while those at the top seek alternatives. Initially, transport companies may be able to absorb higher fuel costs. However, this can only be done by lowering profits. And since this risks investor-flight, it cannot go on for any length of time. Sooner or later, prices have to rise. As transport costs increase, so some consumers simply stop buying. Unfortunately, taken in total, these marginal customers provide the income that allows the transport companies to be profitable.

In a country that operates a just-in-time food supply in which we are just nine meals from starvation, the prospect of the global transport system becoming intermittent or even just much more expensive should be a matter of great concern. However, for the most part we – and our political leaders – simply assume that the supermarkets will be able to provide us with cheap food forever.

All of our critical infrastructure – the grid, transportation system, water and sewage, banking, communications, etc. – depend upon marginal additional customers to maintain profitability. We might, for example, be annoyed by people posting cat videos or playing Candy Crush Saga on social media. However, without this activity – and the money that they pay for it – the fibre optic and wifi communications system would become unprofitable[12]. Higher energy costs on the one hand increase the cost of maintaining the communications system, and on the other hand cause poorer consumers to reduce their discretionary spending. The result is familiar – communications companies lose profitability and must ultimately increase prices. This drives even more consumers away, further reducing profitability and prompting investor flight.

As a society, we might arrive at the conclusion that this critical infrastructure is too important to be allowed to fail. We might make the political choice to, in effect, force society to divert energy and resources away from discretionary spending in order to keep the infrastructure operational. In practice we would either:

---

[12] The US Department of Homeland Security lists a total of 16 critical infrastructure systems: The chemical sector, commercial facilities, communications, critical manufacturing, dams, defence industrial base, emergency services, energy, financial services, healthcare and public health, information technology, nuclear power and waste, transportation, water and sewage. (www.dhs.gov/critical-infrastructure-sectors). One may assume that the UK government's civil contingencies planners have identified similar systems here. Importantly, all of these systems depend upon an uninterrupted supply of energy to function. However, in both countries the focus for planning is on external threats such as terrorism or a cyber-attack rather than the internal threat of operating companies failing to invest in maintenance and future capacity.

o Provide state subsidies to the operating companies (as we currently do with our rail network)

o Run the infrastructure on a not-for-profit basis (as we do with Welsh Water)

o Nationalise the infrastructure and pay private companies to operate it (as we do with London Transport)

o Nationalise the infrastructure and run it directly (as we used to do with British Telecom and the Post Office).

In the face of our leaders' almost religious belief in the infallibility of the free market, we may never get to make this choice. Even if we do, it is important to understand that it will have to be taken at a time where government and public services are themselves under pressure as a result of increasing energy prices. Subsidising infrastructure is likely to have to involve removing funding from a raft of public services in the face of significant public protest.

For the past three centuries our access to cheap and easily available energy has allowed our global economy to grow in complexity. Nobody planned to do this. Complexity simply increased in response to the problems our economy threw up as it grew. Each of the problems we face today is a consequence of the "solutions" that were put in place to deal with yesterday's problems. To give two examples:

1. From the mid-19th century, technological developments demanded that our economies produce an educated workforce in which a growing proportion of the workforce were literate and numerate, while a smaller proportion were educated to a high enough level to turn out the technicians, engineers and academics required to maintain growth. This tended to result in state-funded public education systems that mirrored the industrial economies that they were established to serve.

In time, these education systems encountered two key problems. First, and most obvious, selection bias tended to favour the sons and daughters of the elite rather than the people best suited and endowed to become the best engineers, technicians and academics. This resulted in the demand – which remains unrealised even today – for "equality of access". Second, the system is reactive when the economy needs it to be proactive. That is, it turns out engineers, technicians and academics ideally suited for the economy *as it was a decade ago*! The main response to both of these problems has been to broaden the base – if we push enough students through the industrial state education systems, hopefully a sufficient number of good, forward-looking engineers, technicians and academics will come out the other end… we hope.

So long as the economy had access to a growing supply of cheap energy, it could afford to educate a growing proportion of the population to degree level and beyond.

It could also afford to let large numbers drop out at the bottom. However, as energy supplies dwindle and become more expensive, this becomes much less affordable. Society cannot afford to support large numbers of illiterate and innumerate adults. Nor can we bear the costs of producing over-educated but under-used graduates. Pushing more than half the population through university becomes an unproductive overhead, effectively draining energy and resources away from more important sectors of the (shrinking) economy.

2. From the early 20th century improvements in public health and hygiene, and later in medicine, have allowed a much greater number of us to survive childbirth and to avoid death or disability in the first five years of life. From this pool of survivors, a much greater number have survived to see their hundredth birthday. This has helped push the average life expectancy up above eighty years for women and just below eighty for men.

On the positive side, this additional population provided the human labour to grow the economy from a primarily rural one in 1900 to an advanced urbanised one in the early 2000s. Without these additional people, it would have been extremely difficult for new industries to secure the workforce they needed to expand. On the negative side, an aging population is placing strains on the system that we have never encountered before. Most obviously, providing long term pensions (and related benefits) that were based on the belief that most people would only live for five years past retirement, means allocating money (essentially claims on future energy) away from the productive economy. Other negative consequences include the additional costs of health and social care services, as far more people develop non-fatal long-term illnesses; the cost of informal caring arrangements; the need for sheltered, residential and nursing homes; and the (unmet) need to build more housing for younger workers.

Whether we perceive things like education and healthcare as a good or bad thing is not my point here. The issue is, rather, whether we can afford them – at least in their current form – in the event of the *net energy* available to society falling. The current answer is that we do not really know. Very few people have tried to calculate the energy costs of the various social programmes and public services that have grown up as solutions to previous problems in the economy. However, those academics who have tried to calculate the EROI needs of our society suggest that in the very near future, many of the services we have taken for granted will begin to break down.

The Money Problem

One academic who has begun the process of calculating the energy needs of our economy is professor Charles A.S. Hall, who has made a broad calculation of the EROI costs of a range of economic and social needs within the modern US economy. Remembering that the EROI from unconventional oil is less than 5:1 and that the best of the renewables – onshore wind – comes in at 20:1 (but must be built in vast quantities) we can see potential problems for areas like the arts, healthcare and education as EROI falls across the economy:

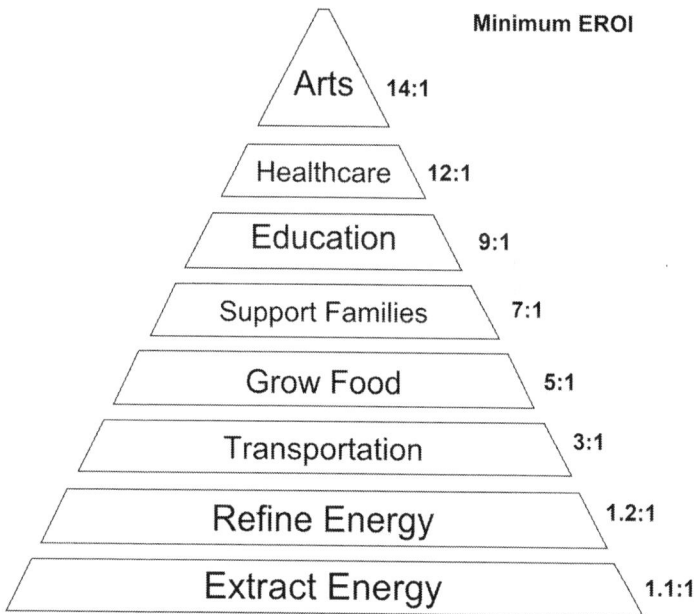

Minimum EROI

Arts — 14:1
Healthcare — 12:1
Education — 9:1
Support Families — 7:1
Grow Food — 5:1
Transportation — 3:1
Refine Energy — 1.2:1
Extract Energy — 1.1:1

The problem is worsened because we do not use energy directly as a currency. Over hundreds of years we have developed a debt-based money system to provide the lubricant for economic transactions. Money – as a payment – becomes a proxy for the energy embodied in a good or service that is sold. Money – as savings – becomes a claim on future energy; either directly when we buy food or fuel, or indirectly when we buy goods and services that have embodied energy.

Our global money system (like all other "solutions") is a response to the problems that arose in our complex global economy. Solutions like credit and limited liability were devised to allow the development of large scale enterprises that simply could not have been funded out of existing income, and whose risks would have deterred all but the most reckless investors. However, these "solutions" have become problems in a financialised economy in which limited liability companies can over-borrow without personal risk to shareholders, and in which banks can create new money out of thin air:

> "In the modern economy, most money takes the form of bank deposits. But how those bank deposits are created is often misunderstood: the principal way is through commercial banks making loans. Whenever a bank makes a loan, it simultaneously creates a matching deposit in the borrower's bank account, **thereby creating new money**."[13]

The real problem with using money as a proxy for energy is that *useful* energy is finite whereas debt-based money is – theoretically – infinite. When the money supply is greater than the available energy in an economy, the result is inflation. At various points in our history people have sought to work around this problem by tying money to precious metals, particularly gold. Since gold is rare and difficult to obtain, gold-backed money cannot easily expand beyond the energy available to an economy. The one notable occasion when it did – when the Spanish empire plundered the gold of the Americas, the result was catastrophic inflation and the ultimate collapse of the empire. Until relatively recently, our own global economy was based on a gold standard too. However, as the British Empire collapsed in the 1930s, it was forced off the Gold Standard. After World War Two, the USA established the modern system in which the US Dollar was backed by gold, and all other currencies were valued against the Dollar. However, in 1971, after the USA had abused its position to deficit finance its war in Vietnam, the Nixon administration was forced to abandon the gold standard. Since that time, all global currencies have been free-floating, fixed, nominally, to a US Dollar that is fixed to nothing at all. The result has been a massive expansion of credit-based money in both the public and, especially the private sectors of the economy.

[13] Michael McLeay, Amar Radia and Ryland Thomas. *Money creation in the modern economy*. Bank of England Quarterly Bulletin 2014. (my emphasis).

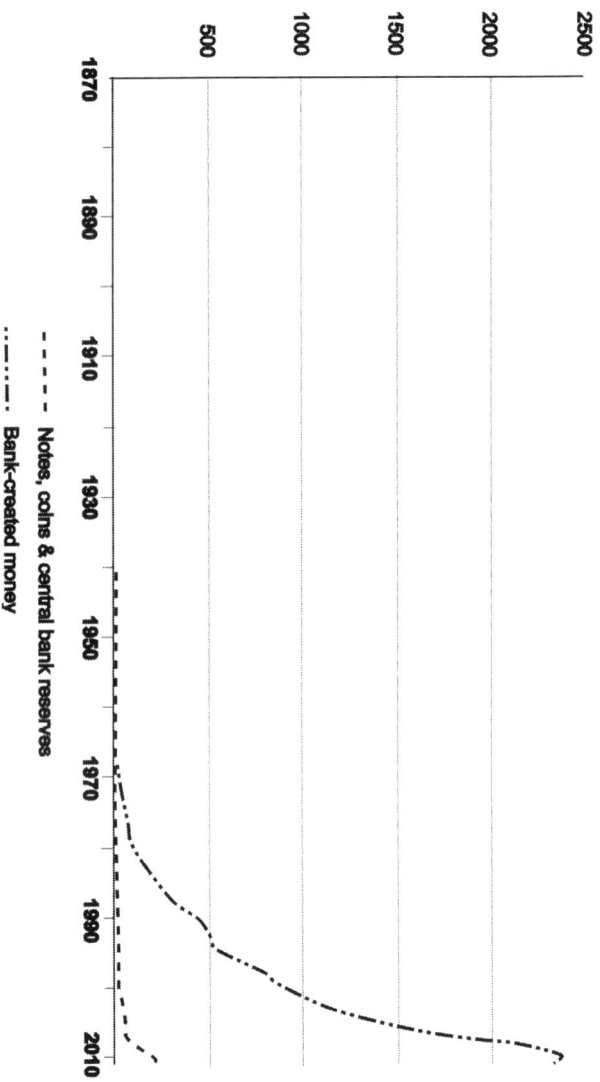

UK Money Supply 1870-2010, (£ billions)

Notes, coins & central bank reserves

Bank-created money

In this *fiat*[14] currency system there are huge pressures to expand debt. Politicians use debt as the most convenient way of bridging the gap between the unrealistic and unfunded promises they make during election campaigns and the actual income of the treasury. The banking industry makes its profits from the debt it creates, so it goes out of its way to invent new ways of extending credit to as many individuals and companies as the state will let it get away with. The public are also duplicitous in this, since we vote for politicians that offer us these unfunded promises; and we take out the loans the banks offer to us. However, the public are less guilty because we are often unable to avoid debt. For example, if the banks decide to make money by offering mortgages to people with smaller deposits, the result (in the absence of a massive house building programme) is that house prices increase. Where this is the backdrop for a family that is relocating to take up new employment, there is little choice but to borrow – and buy – at the going rate.

If energy was an infinite resource whose use we could grow exponentially, this massive expansion of credit would not be a problem. Our economy would always be growing at a faster rate than our credit was expanding. As a result, future generations would always be able to pay off *our* debts. If, however, we have finite fuel from which to generate energy, and obtaining that fuel is becoming more difficult year on

---

[14] Latin, meaning "let it be so". The two things that give "value" to a fiat currency are the law forcing traders to accept it as a legal tender and the law requiring that it must be used to pay taxes.

year, then our ability to keep printing new money (in the form of new loans) becomes a serious problem.

If we can no longer depend upon continuous economic growth, and, indeed face a future in which constrained energy supplies force us to shrink whole areas of the economy, then it will be impossible to pay off debts. This, in turn, makes investing impossible, since the return would always be less than the investment. Pensions[15], for example, only work because we take for granted that the savings we invest will grow over time. Mortgages, too, assume that our incomes will increase over time so that repayment becomes easier over time. Once the opposite conditions apply, the system fails. Only an idiot will save money where the expectation is that their savings will be worth less at the end. Nobody will take out a mortgage if they expect the repayments to become increasingly difficult to meet over time.

The ratio of money to available energy in our current economy has a similar effect to the ratio of money to gold in earlier times. So long as money corresponded to gold, the economy would be stable. However, Kings and Emperors always had an incentive to cheat by putting less gold and silver into the coins, snipping the edges off coins, or even making coins out of base metals then giving them a

---

[15] Both the pensions and insurance industries depend upon an interest rate of 5 percent or more, as a result they are seriously undermined by the prolonged period of 0.5 percent interest rates.

thin wash of gold or silver. The result was that the King – buying at the face value of the coins – got rich while the people – facing inflation – got poorer: a classic transfer of wealth. With the development of banks, bankers could get in on the act too. Bankers could provide safe storage for gold, providing depositors with a credit note with which they could reclaim their gold at a later stage. Eventually, these *banknotes* came to be treated as "good as gold", and people began to use them as money. But this provided the means for bankers to cheat. There was nothing to stop the bankers issuing more bank notes than they had gold to back them. However, in practice when money is debased or when too many promissory notes are issued, people experience inflation; rising prices, although in reality it is the decreasing value of the money itself. When this happened, people would return to the bank to get their gold. This would lead to a run on the bank and result in it going bust.

In a world of fiat currency and electronic money, the mechanisms are different but the practice is essentially the same. Banks create money out of thin air every time they make a loan. No money is lost from any account anywhere else in the system. No saver has money deducted from their account. All that happens is that the bank adds an amount corresponding to the loan as an asset in its account books. The problem, however, is that there is nothing to back this additional money up. So the banks get richer and the public is impoverished by the practice.

In the modern world, debt-based money allows for a huge misallocation of future energy because the needs of the economy and the needs of wealthy individuals are different. For example, the economy *needs* massive investment in sustainable energy. This is no longer a question of fossil fuels versus renewables; this is about every form of energy we can generate… including nuclear. However, at our current state of knowledge and technical ability, this demands huge investment in research and development in such areas as:

○ Carbon capture and storage to mitigate climate change

○ Battery technology to overcome intermittency in renewable energy generation

○ Improved efficiency and life expectancy of renewables

○ Nuclear waste processing and storage.

Instead, what research and development funding we do have is being used to deplete our supplies of fossil carbon more rapidly in a vain attempt to maintain output. Meanwhile, the wealthy elite have been able to waste vast amounts of money on luxury items that will be useless in an age of expensive energy. Indeed, the top ten percent of the world population – which includes almost everyone in the UK[16] -

[16] If your income is above the UK minimum wage, you are in the top 10 percent of people who have ever lived on this planet.

have been enjoying a standard of living that would have been the envy of Kings in days gone by. And very few of us are prepared to sacrifice even a fraction of our lifestyle *today* to mitigate problems that we will have to face in future. This locks us – and the politicians and bankers – into a system that demands that we print additional money (essentially claim additional future energy) in order to maintain our lifestyles. And we will keep doing this until we get the energy equivalent of the old fashioned run on the bank when it became clear there was not enough gold (energy) to meet all of the claims.

Ultimately, the global banking system will crash simply because there is not enough energy to back up all of the claims upon it. The result will be to wipe out billions of Pounds, Euros, Dollars and Yen. Only then will we realise that we no longer have the means to overcome our energy shortage. We will *know* how to make wind turbines, solar panels, tidal barrages and nuclear reactors; but we will no longer have the *means* to build them in sufficient numbers to save our way of life.

Diminishing Returns

The economics of technology follows a particular, well-defined trajectory. Initially, the technology is expensive (and often turns out to be of relatively poor quality). At this point, sales depend on the people that the marketing industry refers to as "early adopters". These are the people that buy goods solely because they are new. They are untroubled by cost or quality. Their goal is to have the new technology *before anyone else.*

Without the early adopters, technology would never develop beyond the science laboratory. The rest of us simply would not buy it. The majority of us prefer to wait until a technology has been tried and tested before we will consider adopting it. Indeed, there is a significant minority that simply refuses to adopt technology unless they are forced to – this is the group that only has i-pods because we stopped making cassette tapes.

As the vast majority of us buy into a new technology, we have two impacts on the market. First, and most obviously, we bring down prices. The firms selling technology are able to use volume sales to reduce unit production costs. A proportion of these savings are passed on to consumers in lower prices which, in turn drive further sales. Second, and less obviously, wider sales allow manufacturers to identify faults and to make improvements to the technology so that as prices fall, quality increases.

The early roll out of a new technology produces increasing returns. Each input to manufacturing produces an improvement in quality and a fall in production costs, allowing prices to fall and increasing consumer demand. However, there comes a point at which making additional changes to the technology and the production process ceases to produce returns. Improvement is still possible. It is just that the cost of the improvement does not deliver sufficient benefit to make the change worthwhile. This is what is known as *diminishing* returns. When diminishing returns impact on the production of a technology – whether it be a car, a television, a phone or a toaster – manufacturers do two things. First, they stop making improvements. The quality and price of the technology stabilises. Second, they seek to develop an alternative new technology. Hence, flat screen TVs replaced cathode tube TVs, and LED TVs are replacing older flat screens.

Thus far, this process has operated for at least three centuries. As each technology has reached the point of diminishing returns, we have simply moved on to a new, improved and, crucially, cheaper technology. So, for example, canals took over from horse-drawn coaches, railways replaced canals, cars and trucks replaced trains. Because this has always happened in the past, we assume that the same trajectory will be followed with technology in the future.

Alarmingly, we tend to see energy generation in general and oil production in particular as following the same trajectory. Certainly past experience would appear to confirm this. Three hundred years ago, we depended almost entirely on renewable energy – human and animal muscles, wood burning, water wheels and windmills. From the late-eighteenth century we began to add coal to the mix – gradually improving the process by which we obtained coal, allowing greater volumes to be obtained at a lower price. From the mid-nineteenth century we began to add oil to the energy mix. As with coal, incremental improvements in production techniques have allowed us to massively increase production *without* needing to increase prices. In exploring the world for oil, we also found massive deposits of natural gas, which we added to the mix in a similar manner to oil – ramping up production while maintaining low prices.

In the 1950s, we were promised that nuclear power would follow a similar trajectory. While the early reactors were inefficient and costly, as countries around the world adopted nuclear, the technology would improve significantly, while the cost of electricity would fall. However, it turned out that the cost of nuclear power could not be made economical – when the cost of building power stations and the cost of processing waste were added, nuclear could not compete with coal and gas fired electricity generation. Most nuclear power stations today owe their existence to the military need for processed uranium for nuclear weapons, which prompted the government subsidies that made the plants viable. For nuclear power to be economically viable in its own right, the cost of gas, oil and coal needs to rise significantly.

Similar problems are being encountered today with renewable energy generation. Solar, wind and tidal energy depend on concentrating diffuse energy. In practice, this means that a huge land/sea area must be given over to renewables if we are to generate sufficient energy to make them worthwhile. This, in turn, means that the initial investment costs required to build industrial-scale electricity generation leaves renewables struggling to compete with coal, oil and gas generation whose power plants and infrastructure are already in place. The added difficulty with renewables is the confusion about whether they are meant to *add* to our energy mix or whether they are meant to *replace* fossil carbon generation. For the last three centuries we have *added* new forms of energy generation. We can also, relatively easily, *add* renewables to the mix. However, if the aim is to *replace* most or all of the electricity we generate from fossil carbon, the task is immense. In the UK we would need to cover up to two-thirds of our land area with wind turbines and solar panels to even begin to replace our existing fossil carbon generation. Even then, we would need to open several new nuclear power stations and develop sea-based wind farms, tidal barrages and wave power generators. This is all *technically* possible, but it would involve an enormous redeployment of the capital, labour, resources and *energy* that are currently being used elsewhere in the economy.

We have a problem with the technological development trajectory that we have assumed for three centuries. Until now we have offset diminishing returns on older technology by inventing and deploying new technology. In energy generation this only *appeared* to be the trajectory because coal is a massively concentrated source of fossilised solar power, and because gas and oil are even more concentrated than coal. But this is where the trajectory breaks down. Certainly uranium offers us a highly concentrated energy source. However, it turns out that the investment required to generate electricity from uranium is too expensive to make nuclear power economically viable. The same is true for different reasons with renewables. In order to develop electricity generation from renewables at a scale that would allow us to overcome diminishing returns from fossil carbon generation, we would require the kind of economic disruption that only tends to be acceptable in wartime. Even then, it is far from clear that we have the resources, energy and technical ability to develop renewable energy on an industrial scale.

The problem is that we have been experiencing diminishing returns in the oil and gas industry for more than a decade:

> "According to Schlumberger the industry's capital expenditures for oil and gas have grown by about 12% annually over the last decade. Oil and gas production grew less than 2% a year in the same period."

The reasons for this concern the way we have followed the low-hanging fruit approach to extraction. Quite simply, we

[17] Stephen Leeb. 6.5.13. *Dangerous Times As Energy Sources Get Costlier To Extract.* Forbes.
http://www.forbes.com/sites/greatspeculations/2013/06/05/dange rous-times-as-energy-sources-get-costlier-to-extract

began by extracting the easy oil and gas that was just below the surface of the land in areas where we already had transport infrastructure. When we exhausted this, we moved on to more remote areas. Then we started drilling beneath the sea, venturing out into ever deeper waters and increasingly hostile climates. Even in the Arabian Peninsula and the Persian Gulf, oil producing states are now extracting oil at sea as the land-based oil fields deplete. Technologies that allow oil and gas extraction from shale and tar sands became viable when oil prices rose above $100 per barrel at a time when governments were holding interest rates at close to zero.

In the absence of an alternative energy source to replace a fossil carbon industry beset by diminishing returns, the question is whether the global economy can continue to bear the additional costs.

Beyond Supply & Demand

In economics the "price discovery mechanism" is based on the market's ability to balance supply and demand:

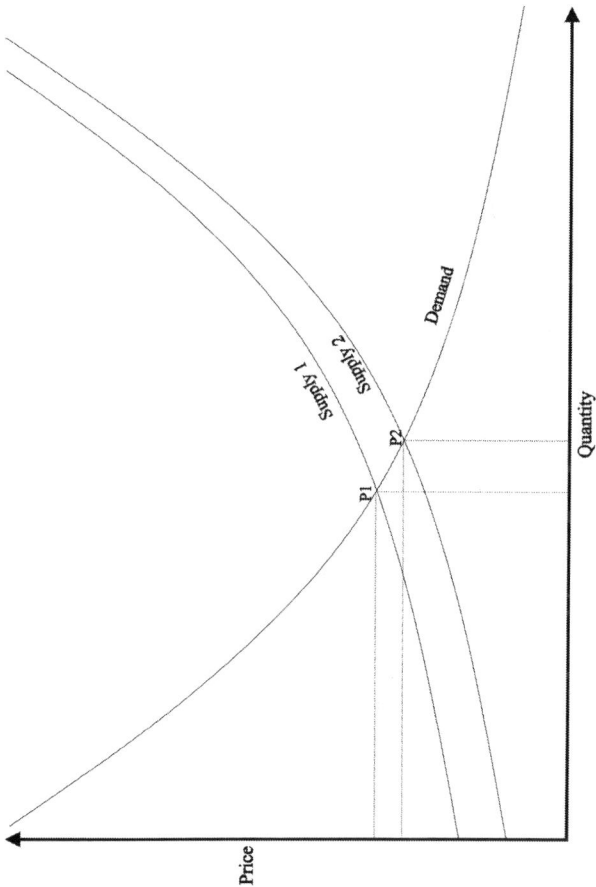

Where there is high demand but low supply of a good or service, prices will be high. Where there is low demand but high supply, prices will be low. Of course, if prices fall too low, the whole enterprise will become unprofitable; investors will walk away and the business will fold. On the other hand, if prices rise too high, then potential consumers will no longer be able to buy. The result will be a classic "crisis of overproduction" in which the business ends up with finished products that it cannot sell. There are several responses to this that make sense for individual businesses but that are catastrophic for the economy as a whole. Firms can seek to lower the cost of components and raw materials by forcing suppliers to absorb the cost of cutting prices. However, since the main cost to most firms is the cost of labour, most will seek to:

○ Cut employees' pay

○ Cut employees' hours.

This may work if only one business is seeking to cut its costs. However, if overproduction has become a problem across the economy, all these measures achieve is a further decline in consumers' spending power as workers are less able to buy goods and services.

Fortunately, until now these periodic crises have tended to be relatively short-lived. This is because competition provides a strong motive to develop technological improvement and substitution. Technological improvement involves deploying technology in a manner that increases labour productivity. That is, it allows a business to produce more of its goods or services without the need to increase its workforce. This effectively lowers the cost – and the market price – allowing the business to supply consumers who previously could not afford the price. Substitution acts in a similar way on components and raw materials. If, for example, a business had been using a particular metal in the manufacture of its widgets, but the cost of that metal had risen to the point that the cost of the widgets was too high, it might be that an alternative metal could be used to lower the price of the widgets once more. Alternatively, it might be that recycling might make the metal cheaper than continuing to mine it. Either way, the result is that the price of widgets falls back to a level at which consumers will buy them once more.

Energy is different. Unfortunately, economists tend not to know this. Energy cannot be manufactured (or, indeed, destroyed). All that we can do is to convert energy from one form into another. However, whenever we convert energy in order to use it in the economy, we *always* lose a proportion as unusable heat that radiates into space. Ultimately, this means that we will run out of usable energy at some time in future. It also means that we will cook the planet at some point in the next 400 years if we continue to grow the economy at the modest rate of 2.5 percent. This has nothing to do with climate change; it is simply that the accelerating rate at which we are producing heat energy is greater than the rate at which it can be radiated into space. Emitting large volumes of carbon dioxide (which acts like a blanket to prevent heat dissipating into space) into the atmosphere merely accelerates the speed at which we boil ourselves to death. However, the more immediate concern for us is that once we have converted the stored, chemical energy locked up in fossil carbon, it has gone forever. If fossil carbon were an infinite resource, this would not pose a problem – beyond finding a way of keeping the planet cool. But, fossil carbon is the product of very particular climate conditions that prevailed at the time of the dinosaurs, and of millions of years of geological processes that "cooked" the coal, oil and gas we use today – it is a once-and-for-good gift (and curse) to humanity.

Geologists estimate that we are roughly halfway through the Earth's oil deposits. However, we still have a problem. First, much of the remaining oil is located in fields that have already passed peak production. Where oil used to gush out of these fields under its own pressure, we now have to deploy increasingly sophisticated – and costly – techniques to pump out the remaining oil. Second, all of the big, easy to reach oil fields have been discovered. The smaller and harder to reach deposits are now being developed, but these require a much greater energy investment to obtain. Third, with our current state of knowledge and technical development, much of the oil that is left would be too expensive to obtain and is likely to have to remain underground. Fourth, growing concerns about climate change are adding to the costs of extracting more fossil carbon. Political developments such as the use of carbon taxes would make the cost of further extraction uneconomic.

So we have a limited and falling supply of oil (and similar problems with gas and coal) that cannot be profitably reversed. Technological fixes such as horizontal drilling and hydraulic fracturing can boost oil and gas production, but they depend upon historically high oil and gas prices to make them profitable. As such, while they may boost supply, they cannot lower costs. Michael Kumhof[18] from the International Monetary Fund Research Department argues that the price of oil will need to steadily rise to at least $200 per barrel by 2020 if unconventional oil – shale, tar sands, deep water and Arctic drilling – is to be deployed to replace conventional crude oil. Even then, it is doubtful that unconventional oil can be extracted fast enough to replace the volumes of conventional oil that we have come to rely on.

Unfortunately, ten out of the last 11 economic crashes – including the great crash of 2008 – were preceded by a rise in oil prices. Because oil fuels almost all of the transport in the global economy, any increase in the price of oil results

[18] *Peak Oil - Oil Prices Need to Double in a Decade.* www.youtu.be/4ZmJKvnCFFE See also: Kumhof, M. and Muir, D. 2012. *Oil and the World Economy: Some Possible Futures.* IMF Working Paper.

in increased prices across the economy. Products (such as plastics) that are made from oil receive a double whammy since in addition to the increase in transport costs, their raw material costs increase too. Food security is a particular problem because the entire global food infrastructure is based around oil. Agriculture depends upon petroleum-powered vehicles both for growing and transporting crops. Less obviously, it depends upon oil-based fertilisers, pesticides and herbicides. Moreover, in many regions it also depends on oil-powered irrigation pumps. So a key result of an increase in oil prices is that global food prices will increase rapidly.

When the oil price spiked in 2006, governments in the developed countries raised interest rates in an attempt to curb the inflation that they believed was the biggest threat to their economies. Higher interest rates immediately hit household spending as millions of people were forced to set aside a much greater proportion of their income to service their debts. This was a particular problem for millions of mortgage holders in the USA, who had been encouraged to take out so-called sub-prime mortgages which appeared to be affordable at a low interest rate. As these mortgage holders fell behind with their payments, and ultimately defaulted, the banks began to fall back on the default insurance vehicles they had created in an attempt to offset the risks of issuing sub-prime mortgages. However, it turned out that the credit default swaps were effectively useless, and banks were forced to eat the losses.

In this way, the 2006 oil price spike fed through into the banking collapse of 2008 and the continuing government bailouts and zero percent interest rate policies that continue to this day. This must raise a question about the likely impact of $200 per barrel oil in the future. Given that $100 per barrel oil caused the global economy to crash, we cannot be confident that the economy can absorb oil prices at anywhere near that level in future.

One place to examine what might happen to oil in the near future is to examine the demand side of the equation. Generally, when the price of something rises the volume of sales drops as poorer consumers can no longer afford to buy. When this happens, it creates a market for any competitor who is able to offer the same or similar goods or services at a cheaper price. If, however, there is no alternative, then the whole enterprise risks entering a vicious downward spiral:

○ Increasing prices lead to poorer consumers dropping out

○ To continue to be profitable with fewer consumers (falling demand), the enterprise must raise prices

○ Price rises cause even more consumers to drop out

○ Fewer consumers cause prices to rise once more.

And on it goes.

However, in the real world, things are not quite so straightforward. Rising prices result in reduced demand, but this creates overproduction. The enterprise is left with products that cannot be sold. Faced with this, most businesses will have some kind of fire-sale; selling the surplus for whatever price they can get in order to cut their losses. This is what has occurred in the oil industry since late 2014. The massive surplus of oil in the USA resulting from the fracking boom was only made possible by high oil prices (and vast sums of quantitative easing money looking for the promise of a high rate of return). However, global demand for oil has been flat for most of the period following the 2008 crash. As a result, by 2014, the world was oversupplied with oil. With most of the oil producing states dependent upon the income they receive from oil exports for running their domestic economies, the result was the equivalent of a fire-sale. OPEC refused to turn the taps off, and the US shale oil companies could not afford to stop pumping. The inevitable result was that oil prices fell dramatically.

While the fall in oil prices was largely welcomed by economists and politicians, it hid an alarming longer-term threat. With oil at less than $70 per barrel almost all of the unconventional oil that has not already been drilled is uneconomical. Investors have been pulling out in droves. This means that when demand eventually picks up there will be insufficient supply to meet it. Once the current oversupply has been used up, we face oil shortages and even higher prices.

What this suggests is that we have reached a point at which the supply and demand price mechanism no longer operates. The supply side requires prices of at least $100 per barrel – rising to $200 per barrel in the next five years – in order to secure the investment to maintain production. However, on the demand side prices rising above $70 per barrel trigger a fall in demand and threaten to bring about a new recession.

With both supply and demand failing, the open global market for oil may well begin to break down. On the one hand, oil producing countries may prefer to enter into longer-term bilateral agreements to supply oil to one or more importing countries as this will guarantee a degree of price stability no longer possible on open markets. On the other hand, faced with falling supplies and greater domestic demand, oil producing countries may decide to slow production and restrict exports in order to maintain a degree of energy security. In both cases – and they are not mutually exclusive – the result is that countries without adequate oil supplies will struggle to secure them on the open market.

Energy Security

Recently, the former First Minister of Wales, Rhodri Morgan reflecting on changes since the heyday of Thatcherism observed that:

> "The other huge change since 1983 is that the North Sea Oil bonanza is over. Back then, whoever was running the Government had this amazing ability to spend oil revenues. Governments could afford things. They didn't have to worry about where the next few quid was coming from. The Falklands War was eminently affordable. Paying the cost of the rocketing unemployment benefit bill, as dole queues doubled, then trebled, wasn't a problem. [But] North Sea oil and gas are now in the end-game phase."[19]

In fact, North Sea oil peaked in 1999. Since then oil production has fallen year on year. The UK is once again an oil importing country. And while some politicians fantasise about hydraulically fracturing the Home Counties, the reality is that the UK will never again be self-sufficient in oil and gas.

Nor can the UK easily reopen the coal mining industry that was destroyed in the mid-1980s. In 2012, UK coal production was *lower* than it had been at the height of the Miners' Strike of 1984/5. It would take a massive capital investment, a vast re-skilling of the labour force and a high

[19] *Can the UK learn to cope without oil? Rhodri Morgan asks the big question the next government will really face.* Western Mail. 18 April 2015.

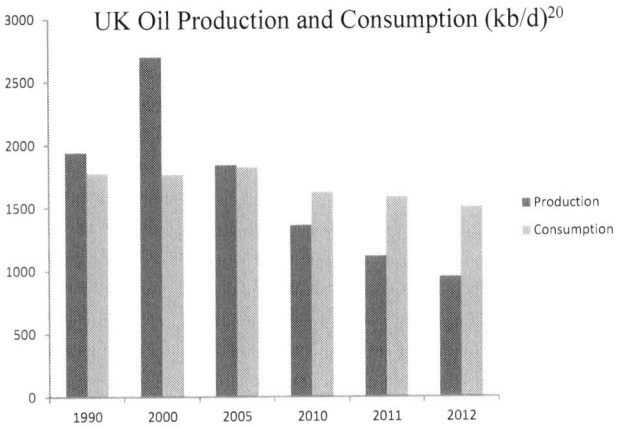

UK Oil Production and Consumption (kb/d)[20]

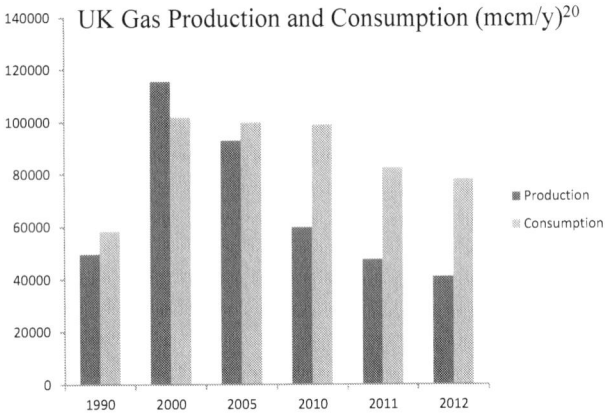

UK Gas Production and Consumption (mcm/y)[20]

[20] International Energy Agency. 2014. *Energy Supply Security 2014 (Part 2: Chapter 4)*

degree of public goodwill that is unlikely to be forthcoming, to bring coal back into production on a scale that would allow it to replace falling oil and gas production.

It is also worth pointing out that UK oil and gas consumption since 2005 has been dampened by the effects of the 2008 crash and the long depression that has followed it. Were the UK economy to have been growing at the desired 3 percent per year, demand would have been significantly higher, leaving the UK even more dependent upon imports and subject to shortages and price hikes in the event of generalised increase in global growth[21].

This highlights a feature of peak oil that few commentators (on both sides of the argument) take into account. Oil importing countries like the UK face a serious energy security problem. This is because the regions of the world from which they must import a growing proportion of their oil and gas are some of the most violent, dangerous and unstable places on Earth. Ukraine has, on several recent occasions, seen the havoc a sudden (political) interruption of supply can wreak upon an economy. We, too, have experienced this before – although the memory of the OPEC oil embargos in the 1970s has faded somewhat. Nevertheless, the best we can look forward to in future is a newly resurgent OPEC that can use its control of global oil supplies to extract a high price from oil importing countries.

[21] In the face of this, we see why our political leaders grasp at the mirage that is hydraulic fracturing of the relatively tiny shale deposits beneath the UK.

The UK is in a relatively fortuitous position in that its partner in the North Sea – Norway – has a very small population, allowing it to continue to export oil and gas despite its oil fields having peaked. This currently provides the UK with a relatively stable supply for a large proportion of its oil and gas. In 2014, 46 percent of UK oil and 54 percent of gas imports came from Norway. Nevertheless, this still left the UK dependent upon less reliable imports from countries like Libya, Nigeria, Russia and several Gulf States for around half of its imports of oil and gas. As we know to our cost, Libya is on the verge of becoming a failed state; relations with Russia have soured; Nigeria has security issues, and the spread of radical Islamic groups in the Middle East may well spread into the Gulf States in future.

However, this is only one of the energy security threats that face us. The main threat is actually much more benign. Oil exporting countries are using an increasing proportion of the oil and gas they produce to power their own domestic economies. When Qatar – which provides the UK with 26 percent of its gas imports – hosts the football world cup in seven years' time, the industrial-scale air conditioning systems they will have to install in their stadia will be powered by oil and gas. Indeed, all of their cities and buildings, together with their cars and trucks are fuelled with oil and gas that, in years gone by, would have been available for export. Moreover, none of the oil producing states is planning to stop growing – the proportion of oil and gas that have to be diverted into their domestic economy is increasing year on year. Saudi Arabia, for example, is projected to reach the point at which all of its oil is required for domestic use by the late 2020s – i.e. just 15 years from now! That means that *even if* it is able to maintain production rates, in practice its oil exports will deplete. The USA, too, is likely to have to reinstate a ban on oil and gas exports (despite the fracking boom being sold on the idea that the USA would become an exporter once more). The UK is also likely to need to divert all of the remaining North Sea output to meeting domestic energy needs, damaging its already poor balance of payments.

Dubai 1990 and 2010

On the demand side of energy security, the emergence of the so-called BRICS countries – particularly China and India – has also put pressure on supplies. Were China to succeed in its plan to expand its economy by 7 percent per year, its consumption of oil would need to double – overtaking the USA's 18,840,000 barrels per day by 2040. India's consumption of oil is also growing rapidly – although from a much smaller base – as a growing middle class seeks to adopt western lifestyles; particularly through rising car ownership and broader access to air travel.

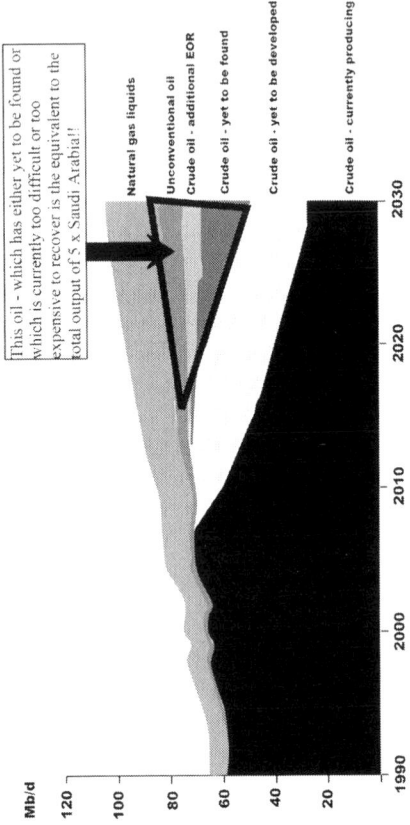

Oil production required to maintain global economic growth

Mb/d

This oil - which has either yet to be found or which is currently too difficult or too expensive to recover is the equivalent to the total output of 5 x Saudi Arabia!!

Natural gas liquids

Unconventional oil

Crude oil - additional EOR

Crude oil - yet to be found

Crude oil - yet to be developed

Crude oil - currently producing

This chart was tucked away in the International Energy Agency's *World Energy Outlook 2008* setting out how oil production would need to be increased to meet increasing demand by 2030.

The chart gives the impression that all is well. However, consider that currently producing oil fields were expected to decline rapidly from 2010[22]. Then consider that in order to maintain production, known but currently undeveloped fields (which require high prices to make them economical) will need to be brought into production. Even so, by 2020 these are also expected to be in decline. Non-conventional oil (tar sands and shale oil) are projected to take up some of the slack. However, the experience of the USA shale industry is that this only works across huge geographical regions, and even then the decline rate is steep – well production falls on average by 80 percent within just three years. The economics of unconventional oil require that prices stay well above $100 per barrel; a price that the global market may be unable to bear.

Natural gas liquids are a by-product of oil production. While they have industrial uses, and can be used to replace oil as a feed base in the chemical industry, they are *not* a replacement for liquid fuels for transportation – i.e. they probably should not be included in the chart as they do not replace like with like.

[22] In fact the global recession has probably delayed the point of decline by four or five years.

Enhanced oil recovery (EOR) is the hope that new technological approaches to recovering oil will allow the industry to revisit oilfields that are well past their peak in order to drain out the remaining oil. There may be something to this insofar as the oldest fields were shut down early simply because they peaked at a time when there was plenty of cheap and easy oil elsewhere. Nevertheless, the recovery of this oil is unlikely to be cheap – if it were, we would already be pumping it out of the ground on the back of the high prices prior to 2014.

Oil fields *yet to be found* are the IEA equivalent of "magic fairy dust" – the vain hope that, despite the most advanced geological surveys of the planet, we may have missed a couple of Saudi Arabia-sized oilfields somewhere. If there were oilfields anywhere near this size, we would have already found them. The only fields left to find will be relatively small, accounting for little more than a few weeks' worth of global demand.

In fact, what the chart is telling us is that we are going to need to find the oil equivalent of somewhere between five and six new Saudi Arabias (the circled area on the chart) within the next 15 years if we are to avoid falling off a very steep cliff. In reality, the US shale and tar sands boom has probably provided sufficient extra capacity to stave this off for a few more years so long as the global economy remains depressed. However, the current low oil prices – largely a result of the US shale bubble – are already beginning to boost economic growth, once again bringing forward the day when global oil production falls for good.

For the UK – no longer self-sufficient in oil and gas – the future looks bleak. Global oil supplies may have already peaked. If they have not, they are likely to do so by 2020. Demand pressures are already growing as the UK has to compete with fast-growing Asian economies for what is left of the world's oil and gas; a pressure that must ultimately drive up prices. Nor can the UK depend upon its current Norwegian oil and gas import cushion lasting forever. As global prices increase and supplies become harder to obtain, the UK will have to compete for these supplies too. Again, that must result in higher prices. Finally, the decline of the west is all too obvious in the USA/UK abject failure to impose their will on Iraq and Afghanistan and, more recently, their inability to prevent the rise of hostile Islamist groups in Iraq/Syria, Yemen and Libya – with the threat that these groups will begin to expand into Saudi Arabia and the Gulf States.

The energy security options available to the UK are limited. Along with their EU partners, the UK has made significant increases in renewable energy generation – which now accounts for 15 percent of the UK's electricity[23]. Household gas and electricity consumption has also fallen in part as a result of national home insulation schemes[24]. This said, it should be noted that the current UK government has

[23] Primarily hydro and wood burning rather than solar and wind.

withdrawn the subsidies that allowed these developments, raising the risk of a serious slowdown in future. It is also worth noting that the government has proved unable to develop a single new nuclear power station in the timescale required to boost energy security. Moreover, the one *planned* new nuclear plant has only been possible by the government agreeing to pay prices that will make the energy generated no cheaper than energy from increasingly expensive imported gas; effectively defeating the object of building it.[25]

Even if the UK were able to develop alternative energy generation, and persuade the population to change their lifestyles in order to save energy, these are only really solutions to falling gas supplies. They provide additional *electricity* but cannot offer an alternative to petroleum for

---

[24] Increasing poverty and government cuts in social security have also caused many families to effectively disconnect themselves.

[25] Just prior to publication, the news broke that there are safety issues with the European Pressurised Reactor design with the result that the development at Hinckley Point has been put on hold, with 400 workers being laid-off. The UK government has also been challenged by the governments of Austrian and Luxembourg for unfairly subsidising the Hinckley Point plant. It is now unlikely that the new plant will be online before 2030. (http://www.resilience.org/stories/2015-06-02/nuclear-decline-in-europe)

the UK transport network. Following the Beeching cuts[26] that decimated the UK rail network in 1963, every UK citizen is now completely dependent upon motorised transport for their life support. The UK produces less than 60 percent of its food, and depends upon a global network of just-in-time supply chains to import and deliver sufficient food to the shops. Without enough oil, and with the high price of whatever oil is still available on the open market, these transport systems will face increasing strain and disruption – and if they become uneconomical, they will break down.

By the time the UK government and its people realise that they have an energy security problem – most probably the day the petrol filling stations stop pumping – we will be decades too late to invest in the large-scale renewable and nuclear power generation that are our only real hope. It takes around 25 years to replace the national vehicle fleet – longer for aeroplanes and ships. Even if there were viable electric vehicles (something that is currently unlikely for large vans and trucks, and impossible for ships and planes), we would need to have begun rolling these out back in 1990. In practice, without the state investing in the infrastructure (advanced battery chargers and/or battery replacement stations) and subsidising the research into and development of the next generation of battery technology, we will remain

---

[26] See for example: http://www.bbc.co.uk/news/uk-21938349

largely dependent upon petrol- and diesel-fuelled vehicles for years to come. But it is far from clear where we are going to find the oil to fuel them.

The Near Future: A World Without Cheap Liquid Fuels

Nobody can predict with any certainty what the world beyond cheap oil will be like. One of the problems with many of the peak-oilers is that they tend to talk about the consequences in apocalyptic terms, as if the entire world will come crashing down around our ears within months of oil production peaking. This is, perhaps, understandable when we consider that the early peak-oilers were oil industry insiders concerned that the world was sleep-walking to a potential catastrophe.

One response to this – one I personally hold to – is that if you want to see what a world without cheap oil looks like, go and look out of your window (or look at a newspaper):

o A million families using food banks is what a world without cheap oil looks like

o The replacement of high-paid/high-skilled employment with low-paid/low-skilled jobs is what a world without cheap oil looks like

o The inability of the developed economies to stimulate economic growth is what a world without cheap oil looks like

o Governments' (including those pursuing austerity policies) failure to avoid running up massive government debts is what a world without cheap oil looks like o The dramatic slowdown in the Chinese economy (which was meant to be the engine for global growth) is what a world without cheap oil looks like

o The multi-trillion pound misallocation to asset bubbles and property speculation (because the real economy has gone into reverse) is what a world without cheap oil looks like.

This is, of course, just the beginning. It is not that we cannot find new oil reserves – it is that we cannot find *enough* new reserves to lower prices. It is not that we cannot pump oil out of the ground; it is that we cannot do it *without increasing prices.* It is not that we cannot find alternatives; it is that we cannot deploy alternatives *quickly* and *cheaply* enough. These trends can only get worse as the amount of oil available to world markets continues to fall[27].

The threat to us all is that we may reach a tipping point at which the critical infrastructure of both the global and national economies breaks down. While we have a largely free market in which billions of economic transactions take place day in, day out, for this to happen we depend upon several "monopoly" systems – these are not so much monopolies in the sense of being owned and controlled by

---

[27] Ironically, the economic pain will be even worse if – as seems likely – increasingly limited energy and resources are diverted to the development, manufacture and installation of renewable energy generation.

a single corporation or government, but rather because there is just the one. I do not have a choice about:

○ Whose sewage system I will flush my waste into

○ Whose grid I will get my electricity from

○ Whose pipes will supply my gas

○ Whose fibre optic cables will handle my communications data

○ Whose banking network will handle my transactions

○ Whose transport system will deliver my food, clothing and household goods

While all of these systems may be run by various companies, and access to them may also be subject to competition, the point is that there is not a substitute waiting in the wings. If the national grid fails, we are without electricity. If the banks collapse, we cannot make even the most basic transactions – such as obtaining cash or paying for our shopping. More worryingly, these systems are not free standing. The electricity grid depends upon the transport system for its engineers to maintain the system. The water and sewage system depends upon the grid for the electricity to run its pumping stations. Without water and sewage, most of our food outlets have to shut for health and safety reasons. Without electricity, communications and the inter-bank system break down.

This matters because each of these systems is only economically viable with mass usage. The end of cheap oil (and gas) puts pressure on mass usage through increasing prices. Most obviously, the increase in energy prices after the 2008 crash has resulted in millions of people effectively disconnecting themselves from the grid. In order to replace the income lost as this group opts out, the energy companies are obliged to increase prices for those who remain. This is, of course, a short-term solution, since it ultimately causes even more people to opt out. Less obviously, there is pressure at the top from high-income families going off-grid. In practice, much of the increase in solar power in the UK has been fuelled by providing government subsidies (through feed-in tariffs) to the relatively affluent middle classes to install solar panels. This process hits the generators from two directions – not only do they lose the income that these households would otherwise have provided, they are also obliged to *pay* these consumers for the privilege. As prices rise, irrespective of what happens to feed-in tariffs, more and more households at the top will have an incentive to generate as much of their own energy as they can. The result of this is that the cost of maintaining and developing the national electricity grid has to fall onto the shoulders of an increasingly squeezed middle.

Of course, there comes a point at which a system as a whole becomes uneconomical. The companies that run the system can only go so far in cutting employees' wages and skimping on maintenance costs. Eventually, falling revenues feed through into falling returns for shareholders and an inability to service corporate debt. When this threat arises – usually some time prior to the company actually becoming unprofitable – investors walk away and banks refuse to lend. When this happens, the companies go broke and the system collapses.

Whether national governments would actually allow energy generators or the grid itself to fail is a moot point. Given their response to failing banks, it is more than likely that they would step in to save the companies and the grid. However, given the huge levels of public debt that have already been added to prop up the banks, and given the austerity being imposed on ordinary people, it may turn out to be both financially and politically impossible to provide bail outs to the energy generators.

Of equal concern is the likely failure on the part of government to see the problem coming and to respond appropriately to it. The fact is that we have incidents in our past that give a flavour both of what the end of cheap oil might do to our critical infrastructure, and of how government might respond:

"In April 2014, in *Exercise Hopkinson*, UK state planners played out a scenario in which a super-storm caused critical damage to the electricity grid in the southwest of England (where Atlantic storms are likely to do the most damage). Two fossil fuel power stations at Indian Queens and Langage are down for planned routine maintenance and cannot be restarted. The

Nuclear plant at Hinkley Point is safely shut down, but will take several days before it can be safely restarted. The result is that Cornwall, Devon and a large part of Dorset are left without power at a time when National Grid workers are struggling to maintain power in the remainder of the UK."[28]

Nor did the scenario stop with millions of people being left without power. Unusually, *Exercise Hopkinson* explored the way in which the collapse of one essential infrastructure network would cascade into other networks. Hospitals would be forced to close as their emergency generators ran out of fuel, resulting in many more deaths. The transport system would fail as vehicles ran out of fuel and could not be refilled because electric fuel pumps no longer worked. Nor could emergency generators be relied on since these, too, depended upon fuel that had to be pumped using electricity. Similarly, the communications system would rapidly fail as phones needed to be recharged. Other critical infrastructure was also found to be at risk. In many areas, water and sewage systems would break down because they depended upon electricity-powered pumping stations. Fire and rescue services would struggle to identify genuine emergencies as alarm systems tripped because of the power

[28] "Britain unprepared for severe blackouts, secret Government report reveals" *Daily Telegraph*. 28th December 2014.
www.telegraph.co.uk/news/earth/energy/11311725/Britain-unprepared-for-severe-blackouts-secret-Government-report-reveals.html

failure. Prisoners in remote jails might have to be released, and criminals on community sentences might abscond as their electronic tags would no longer operate. Panic buying would most likely cause shops to run out of food, with little prospect of restocking in the near future. Paradoxically, dairy farmers would be able to milk by hand (because electric milking plants no longer worked) but would be forced to throw the milk onto their fields (because milk tankers could not get through to collect it). Businesses, too, would be at risk. Business critical incident plans are based on the assumption that most key employees would be available for work. However, in this scenario, quite understandably, many people would put their families' needs above those of their employers. Planners anticipated that just a third of the usual workforce would be available.

The UK government has glossed over *Exercise Hopkinson*. However, the *Daily Telegraph* has access to secret documents from planners who participated in the exercise. These conclude that:

> "Populations are far less resilient now than they once were… There is likely to be a very rapid descent into public disorder unless Government can maintain [the] perception of security… Any central Government response to the crisis may be too slow, arriving after the local emergency resources and critical utility contingency measures had already been consumed."

This is an example of *cascade* – the process whereby a collapse in one critical infrastructure network (the electricity grid) rapidly infects neighbouring critical networks (e.g. water and sewage, communications, transport, hospitals, food). If such a scenario were to play out in the real world, it would seriously challenge the way governments traditionally respond to emergencies.

For the most part, state emergency planning has focused on individual incidents – a terrorist attack here, a flood there. So long as these occur in relative isolation, even a massive event – like the aftermath of Hurricane Katrina in New Orleans – can be localised; preventing a widespread cascade across the economy. However, events that impact on the functioning of critical infrastructure cannot be isolated and require a form of planning and response that is based upon the understanding that the impact of a cascade will be the same, irrespective of which critical network was the first to be impaired. There are several real-world examples of impaired critical network failures resulting in a cascade into neighbouring systems:

On Thursday 7th September 2000 the price of a barrel of oil rose to $35, adding another .02p to the price of petrol in the UK – taking the price at the pump above the iconic £1.00 per litre mark. Angered by the impact on living standards, and taking their cue from a blockade by French farmers, around a hundred farmers and lorry drivers blockaded the Stanlow Shell Oil Refinery in Cheshire. This marked the beginning of eight days of disorder that brought the UK economy to the edge of collapse.

The following day, a "rolling roadblock" by around 100 lorries brought traffic on the A1 to a standstill. On the same day, protesters blockaded the Texaco refinery in Pembroke. At this point, the protesters were seen by the establishment as a minor nuisance. Political leaders were unconcerned. Nothing much seemed to be happening over the weekend, and the first editions of the Sunday papers barely mentioned the protests. However, by the morning of Sunday 10th September a larger than normal number of motorists across the UK – fearful of further protests – began queuing at filling stations in advance of the Monday morning commute. On the same day, English ambulance trusts instructed their drivers to stick to a 55 mph limit on non-emergency calls in order to save fuel.

On Monday 11th, public support for the protests grew, and many more lorry drivers and farmers joined in. There were more rolling roadblocks, including a number through the centre of several cities, bringing many streets to gridlock. Chancellor Gordon Brown publicly refused to give in to the protests. Behind the scenes, however, the Queen had been asked to sanction the use of emergency powers to break the blockades.

By Tuesday 12th, most filling stations in the UK were out of petrol. Those that still had supplies were rationing users – some to just £5.00 worth of petrol each. By Wednesday 13th, just 280 of the usual 3,000 fuel deliveries had been made. Ninety percent of filling stations had no fuel. The remaining ten percent were rationing fuel and prioritising key workers such as firemen and ambulance crews. On the same day, around 200 lorries were driven into the centre of London, where they were parked in the roads, causing gridlock throughout the capital. Across the UK, food rationing was introduced (by supermarket managers) for the first time since the 1950s following panic buying in the supermarkets. There was a national shortage of basic staples like bread and milk. Hospitals were struggling to obtain key medical supplies – for example, the Royal Hull Hospital ran out of stitches[29] for use in operations.

On Thursday 14th, as drivers were forced to leave their empty cars at home and turn to public transport to get to work, bus companies began to limit their services in order to preserve their remaining stocks of fuel. Many businesses were unable to function as key employees could not get into work. Supply chains began to break down as key components were not transported. At this point, Britain was just days away from a catastrophic collapse. Fortunately, later that day the protesters called off their action, claiming that they had made their point.

---

[29] This is an example of how, during a cascade, the unforeseen shortage of a small component part or the absence of a key worker can bring an entire system to a halt.

Most of the protests came to an end on Thursday 14th, but the effects continued to be felt for several weeks afterward. Over the following weekend, as petrol began to get through to the filling stations and food returned to the supermarket shelves, there were outbreaks of panic buying as rumours spread that there would be renewed blockades the following week. Services and firms that ordinarily operate just-in-time supply chains took several weeks to recover as they were forced to transport extra resources and components to make up for the shortfall caused by the protests. Millions of employees who had been unable to get into work for several days were obliged to catch up on the backlog of work before they could get back to normal.

Although, in the end, the impacts of the UK fuel protests were limited, they demonstrated the lack of resilience to the disruption of critical infrastructure. In a country where commuting is a normal part of people's work patterns, the inability to drive and the collapse of a public transport system that lacks capacity to take up the slack had begun to impact other critical networks as key workers were unable to get to their work. For ordinary people, it demonstrated just how vulnerable we are to disruption to the food supply. It also revealed just how ill-prepared the authorities were to cope with a cascade. For example food and fuel rationing, that probably prevented serious hardship, was initiated randomly by shop and filling station managers and not at the direction of the state. Indeed, left to the authorities, by the time rationing had been legally introduced, there would have been nothing left to ration!

The broader point when looking at the fuel protest is that there was a *normal* to return to. Today we would welcome with glee a world in which oil sold for $35 per barrel on world markets, and a litre of petrol could be bought for a pound. When, however, oil prices rise above $100 per barrel, and governments (desperate for tax income) can do little to keep petrol and diesel prices from rising, *normal* becomes a more difficult place to be. UK car ownership and miles driven have fallen since the crash of 2008 as people's incomes have stagnated while prices have increased. This presents a particular difficulty in an economy that is structured to depend upon commuting.

Most ordinary workers are unable to afford to live in the cities where they work – this is especially true in London, where large-scale asset speculation has driven up house prices, forcing ordinary people out of the centre. The result has been that a growing proportion of households' non-discretionary income has to be diverted to funding the daily commute. However, this has occurred at a time when there are other pressures on non-discretionary spending. Food and energy prices have risen since 2008, and a raft of central government austerity cuts to local authorities have resulted in increases to the council tax and an unlawful use of increased parking charges to balance the books. Anyone whose employment depends upon commuting has little alternative but to pay *all* of these increased costs. However, there comes a time when the cost of commuting rises to the point where it is no longer worthwhile. At this point it is only inertia that stops people leaving their jobs and thus keeps the system running.

Millions of people today would be better off settling for a significantly lower-paid job close to home than continuing to commute. The only reason that more people have not chosen to do this is the belief that the economy will return to some kind of pre-2008 *normal* relatively quickly. This said, after seven years, and with little sign of a significant improvement in the economy beyond asset speculation and outside the City of London, this belief is wearing thin.

When oil prices rise once more – as they are bound to do – we will wake up to the loss of capital expenditure that has occurred since prices began to fall in 2014. On the world market, supply will have diminished even as demand begins to pick up. The inevitable result will be higher prices; perhaps even moving toward the $200 per barrel suggested by the IMF researchers. When this happens, government will struggle to mitigate the effect on prices at the pumps, since the state depends upon fuel taxes to mitigate its rising debt levels.

Alternatives to private car ownership are limited. Rail transport is already at capacity, and suffers overcrowding and high prices during peak periods. Moreover, the rail operators are going to face the same kind of rising energy costs as private motorists. Faced with both rising costs and rising demand, but with limited scope to increase supply, the likely response will be increased fares. Bus transport has some slack insofar as private vehicles and drivers could be brought in to supplement existing services. However, for the most part this would be a local rather than a national response. Moreover, the bus operators would also have to pass on at least some of their increasing fuel costs. *Some* employers may be able to improve the situation for *some* workers by allowing more flexibility, encouraging home working, and taking advantage of internet communications to remove the need for travel. However, in terms of critical infrastructure workers, this is likely to be limited – put simply; you cannot fix burst water mains from home or over the internet! The same situation goes for emergency service workers – firefighters, paramedics and nurses – who also play an essential role in the functioning of a modern city. If sufficient numbers of these key workers choose to walk away from commuting, critical systems come under threat. And in a free market in which we may all – at least in theory – choose our employment, there is little that can be done in policy terms to mitigate the problem. Indeed, given the dynamics within companies, we are unlikely even to realise that we have a problem until our critical infrastructure is impacted.

Consider the power outage that hit the northeast of America (Canada and the USA) on 14th August 2003 – which initially, following the attacks on the World Trade Centre just two years earlier, was thought to be a terrorist attack. The true cause was a failure to invest in maintenance. An overloaded power line in Ohio sagged and made contact with a tree growing beneath the line – a tree that should not have been there had routine maintenance been carried out in the years prior to the outage. The resulting overload at the power station triggered a shutdown which cascaded across the networks, resulting in 256 power stations going off grid and leaving 55 million people without power throughout the day. Although power began to be restored during the evening of 14th August, several critical systems – most notably air transport – took several days to restart. The US automobile industry, for example, did not return to full production until 22nd August.

The worker responsible for cutting down the trees beneath power lines is unlikely to be particularly well-paid, nor likely to be viewed as an essential worker. Yet there are thousands of people in similar positions across our critical infrastructure. These are precisely the kind of people who are the first to walk away when the cost of being employed rises above the cost of lower paid work closer to home. And you only notice their absence when the proverbial hits the fan!

The response to the threat of peak oil (in practice peak *cheap* oil) particularly from the oil industry has been to dismiss it as a conspiracy theory. However, this is usually done by misrepresenting the peak oil case. The oil industry position – supported by many politicians and economists – is to claim that the peak oilers (who mostly state the geology case alone) are claiming that the world is *running out* of oil. Since we have at least as much oil in the ground as we have ever used, this is patently absurd. Hence, they claim there is no crisis; nothing to worry about. Indeed, the economists – whose discipline is more religion than science – argue that even a finite resource like oil will never run out because so long as the price rises sufficiently, an alternative will always emerge. This, I fear, is dangerous complacency. We have already witnessed some of the alternatives that emerge when prices rise sufficiently – fracking, the destruction of forests to access tar sands, the threat to the Arctic and the Gulf of Mexico from deep water drilling; all of which require recession-triggering oil prices if they are to break even. Beyond these, what is the future for an oil-importing country like the UK? New nuclear cannot be mobilised in the timescale needed, even assuming the population can be won over. Even windfarms – probably the most effective and benign of our alternatives – face howls of public protest when anyone proposes building them. Installing solar panels and insulating homes should be done. However, most of the world's solar panels are now made in China (in order to keep wage costs down) and will rapidly increase in price once increased oil prices impact on global transport systems. We may not have time to develop our own local production.

Whatever we do, we cannot avoid the impact of increasing oil prices on our transport systems. In practice, if we intend keeping food in the shops, the simple, unavoidable conclusion is that the mass of the population are going to have to stop driving. This means a radical reorganisation of the way our economy operates. It is likely to involve, for example, a shift from car ownership to car hiring and car sharing. Given that most of our cars spend most of their time on our drives or in car parks, this is not so radical a proposition as it first appears. However, it is unachievable so long as the majority of our workplaces insist that people turn up for work at the same time of day; often within the same congested city centres.

Our lifestyles are also going to have to change. It is highly unlikely that our just-in-time global economy supply chains will be able to survive the end of cheap oil. Shipping raw materials from around the globe to the massive Chinese manufacturing plants in order to produce finished goods that must then be shipped back around the globe to sales outlets will become unprofitable. Economies will have to re-localise – things will be made locally or they will not be made at all. But the biggest threat we face is to food supplies. This is because modern agriculture depends upon oil at every stage from preparing the ground to shipping food to the shops. Agricultural production will inevitably fall unless governments steps in to subsidise production – effectively diverting oil from elsewhere in the economy to enable farms to continue to operate machinery. However, much of UK agriculture is geared to export into world markets, while much of the UK's food is imported from around the world. So while – in theory – UK agriculture could produce two-thirds of the UK's food, in practice to achieve this would require a considerable reorganisation of production; something that will be difficult to achieve overnight.

While there are many peak oil commentators who imagine that falling oil supplies and increasing prices will result in an apocalyptic collapse of civilisation, this is highly unlikely. Critical infrastructure will not collapse entirely. Rather, we will move into a period of intermittency – in which things we take for granted such as food, water, sanitation, electricity and communications will suffer outages more frequently and randomly. This, in and of itself, will force us to re-orientate our economy away from the efficiency (and consequent fragility) of the just-in-time globalised model to a much more adaptable and resilient localised economy. Government will play a central role – though not because it will want to. Ideologically, government will hate what it will have to do. But ultimately, for national security reasons government *will* re-nationalise the UK's critical industry for the simple reason that once it becomes unprofitable, there will be nobody else to operate it.

Where Are We Going?

In this guide to peak oil, I have set out the ways in which various peak oil pressures are beginning to impact upon a UK that no longer enjoys the privilege of being an oil exporting country. In the coming years we will find ourselves increasingly dependent upon oil (and gas) produced in regions of the planet that are already volatile and – facing their own economic problems – are likely to become even more dangerous in coming years.

Nor can the UK be sure of even this unreliable supply of oil. With growing demand from fast developing economies such as China and India, demand for oil is increasing fast even as supplies are falling. Moreover, the oil exporting countries are themselves increasingly dependent upon the oil they produce for maintaining domestic economic growth.

These oil security issues are at least as serious as the original geologists' concerns about our rapidly approaching the point at which we can no longer *increase* oil production – a point that technological developments have allowed us to put off for a few years, but only at the cost of huge additional investment in the oil industry which is only economical if oil can be sustained at a high price.

High oil prices trigger recessions as people's discretionary spending is reduced. The austerity policies adopted in the UK in response to recession actually make this worse[30], as

[30] See for example Watkins, T. 2015. *Austerity… will kill the economy.* Waye Forward (Publishing).

millions of families at the bottom of the income ladder are forced to cut even what should be non-discretionary spending – for example, having to make a choice between energy and food. The structural consequence of this is that the cost of maintaining and developing the UK's critical infrastructure *must* fall on an increasingly squeezed middle. This process is, of course, accelerated as oil, gas and coal prices increase on world markets. However, because the economics of critical infrastructure is based on mass consumption, the companies that own and run the infrastructure will be unable to absorb the loss. Initially they will cut back on maintenance, and drive employees' wages down – paving the way for intermittency through both poorly maintained systems and industrial relations problems (including strikes). Ultimately, though, loss of income from the mass market will impact on the companies' ability to raise money from investors or as loans from banks. When this point is reached, the companies will simply close.

We have no alternatives. Unsurprisingly in the wake of Windscale, Three Mile Island, Chernobyl and Fukushima, the British public have refused to countenance any widespread development of nuclear power. Unforgivably, they have been equally vociferous in their opposition to tidal barrages, windfarms and large scale solar farms. And, of course, they object to fossil carbon because of its impact on the environment. The outcome of this opposition to pretty much anything that might generate electricity is that as oil and gas supplies dwindle, we will be left without the energy we need to run our homes and more importantly *our economy.*

Even if we had invested in renewables and nuclear – and there is still good reason to do both – they would not solve the more fundamental problem. We have no liquid fuel alternative to oil. We have a global economy that depends upon massive oil-powered machinery to extract all of the minerals and resources that we depend upon. We have global transport systems that depend upon massive oil-powered container ships and oil-hungry aeroplanes to transport the goods we need around the planet. Our agriculture is oil intensive. The cities that we have built depend upon oil-driven cars, vans and lorries to operate – we now live, work and play in different districts (and often different cities). We cannot maintain this way of life without access to a *growing* supply of *cheap* oil – the very opposite of the *dwindling* supply of *expensive* oil that we now face.

At this point, surely, I am expected to offer some tranquilising greenwash about how solar panels, cavity wall insulation and electric cars are going to save the day. However, we lost that battle when US president Ronald Reagan symbolically tore the solar panels off the Whitehouse roof. Had we begun to introduce renewable energy and researched and developed alternatives to oil-powered vehicles back in the 1980s, we might have had a chance. Our choice not to do so is now coming home to roost. The global economy is coming to an end. Our own way of life is going to be radically different. Worse still, we are entirely unprepared for a world without cheap oil, and most of us – including our political leaders – do not even see the predicament we are in.

So can I offer hope?

As long as we accept that we will have to change the way we live, then yes, I can offer hope. But if you want some technological quick-fix to allow us to keep running our flat screen TVs, our gas-guzzling private cars, our fast-food restaurants and our oil-dependent conspicuous consumption, I am afraid to say that *all* of that is going to go. Hope comes not from "Disney thinking" (where wishing on a star makes your dreams come true) but from the experience of my grandparents' generation. Between 1939 and 1945, that generation faced a predicament equal in its way to the predicament we now find ourselves in. Initially, their political leaders were as out of touch as ours today. However, faced with the emergency, true leaders (from all sides of politics) emerged. More importantly, far from collapsing, public morale rose to the occasion. They learned to grow food and to "make do and mend"; they adapted to a world without petrol. They tolerated but lived with and accepted rationing of food, clothing and furniture. On a positive note, the wartime diet was actually healthier than many of our contemporaries' diets today – the kind of reduction in calories that we are looking at as global supply chains become intermittent should remove most of our self-inflicted obesity. Furthermore, much of the slack can be taken up simply by eating the third of our food that we currently throw away! Unemployment is also likely to be less of a problem, as human labour will have to be deployed to do some of the work currently done by oil-powered machinery. Politics, too, will have to become more democratic, since the kind of change that we will have to undertake can only be achieved if there is genuine consent[31].

When, in 2008, the banking system collapsed, political leaders around the world acted. When the peak oil crisis hits, they will – against their ideological beliefs – act once more. Once they realise that it is not just the living standards of the poor that are at stake, but the survival of the UK economy as a whole, they will mobilise the state to protect our life support systems. However, it will be we, the people, who will ultimately determine the direction that this transition takes. And this is why I have hope – because I belive that ultimately when we, the people, come together in the face of a crisis, we are more than up to the task.

---

[31] As opposed to the current system in which parties can obtain a five-year parliamentary dictatorship on less than 40 percent of the vote.

Also by Tim Watkins*

○ *Austerity - will kill the economy*

○ *Beating Anxiety: A Guide to Managing and Overcoming Anxiety Disorders.*

○ *Depression: A guide to managing and overcoming depression.*

○ *Depression Workbook: 70 Self-help techniques for recovering from depression.*

○ *Distress to De-stress: Understanding and managing stress in everyday life.*

○ *Food for Mood: A guide to healthy eating for mental health. for anyone who is relatively new to cooking.*

○ *Getting to sleep: A guide to overcoming stress-related sleep problem.*

○ *Good Stress - Bad Stress: Rethinking stress management.*

○ *How to Help: A guide to helping someone manage mental distress.*

○ *Helping Hands: How to Help Someone Else Cope with Mental Health Problems.*

* See Tim Watkins' Amazon Author page for details:
www.amazon.com/-/e/B00E0EN9GO

- *No More Panic - A Guide to overcoming panic attacks and recovering from panic disorder.*

- *Smart Fundraising: A guide to fundraising for small charities and community groups.*

- *What's Wrong With Charity? How modern charity practices are undermining communities, democracy and public trust.*

About Waye Forward

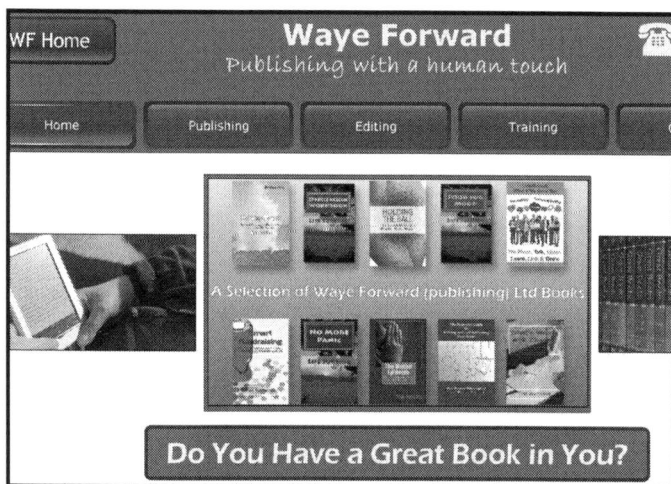

Waye Forward has published a range of books - both clients' books and our own. Now we would like to help you to publish your book too.

We provide a complete package of support:

- ○ Coaching and mentoring
- ○ Editing and proof reading
- ○ Typesetting and cover design
- ○ Publishing

Whether you are just beginning to think about writing a book, or have a finished work that you are happy with, why not let us help you get the best from your work?

publishing.wayeforward.com

27245685R00068

Printed in Great Britain
by Amazon